W9-BCX-399

John K. Conlon
Melissa Giovagnoli

The Power of Two

How Companies of All Sizes Can Build Alliance Networks That Generate Business Opportunities

Jossey-Bass Publishers • San Francisco

Copyright © 1998 by Jossey-Bass Inc., Publishers, 350 Sansome Street, San Francisco, California 94104. All rights reserved. No part of this publication may be reproduced, stored in a retrieval system, or transmitted, in any form or by any means, electronic, mechanical, photocopying, recording, or otherwise, without the prior written permission of the publisher.

Jossey-Bass books and products are available through most bookstores. To contact Jossey-Bass directly, call (888) 378–2537, fax to (800) 605–2665, or visit our website at www.josseybass.com.

Substantial discounts on bulk quantities of Jossey-Bass books are available to corporations, professional associations, and other organizations. For details and discount information, contact the special sales department at Jossey-Bass.

For sales outside the United States, please contact your local Simon & Schuster International Office.

 Manufactured in the United States of America on Lyons Falls Turin Book. This paper is acid-free and 100 percent totally chlorine-free.

Library of Congress Cataloging-in-Publication Data

Conlon, John K., 1952-
    The power of two : how companies of all sizes can build alliance networks that generate business opportunities / John K. Conlon, Melissa Giovagnoli. — 1st ed.
        p. cm. — (The Jossey-Bass business & management series)
    Includes index.
    ISBN 0-7879-0946-7 (cloth)
    1. Strategic alliances (Business) I. Giovagnoli, Melissa. II. Title. III. Series.
    HD69.S8 C662 1998
    658.1'6—ddc21

                                                        98-9057

first edition
HB Printing   10 9 8 7 6 5 4 3 2 1

The Jossey-Bass

Business & Management Series

For my father, James P. Conlon.
His integrity and ability to always do the right thing
endeared him to many.

Contents

Acknowledgments

We wouldn't be sharing this book with you if not for the support of our editor, Cedric Crocker at Jossey-Bass. Through the couple of years it took us to develop and write the book, John and I have thoroughly enjoyed our solid relationship with all the team members at Jossey-Bass.

We would also like to thank Cheryl Greenway, Cedric's assistant and one of our champions, for support above and beyond the call of duty.

Also crucial was our personal editor and agent, Bruce Wexler, who kept our words and ideas flowing as one. His patience and insight into our combined synergies is thoroughly appreciated.

Special thanks also to the many contributors who shared their alliance stories with us, especially Charmaine Stradford and Jocelyn Carter-Miller.

Finally, special thanks to my family, who patiently waited for the completion of this book to regain my full attention.

Hoffman Estates, Illinois   Melissa Giovagnoli
April 1998

I would like to acknowledge the support of many colleagues over the years who worked with me to build alliances. I am especially grateful to Dick Heald and Rose Ann Giordano at Digital Equipment, who provided the support and encouragement I needed to take the risks necessary to create alliances with competitors. I am grateful to the other members of the GESAMT project team: Henry Aldeman, Horst Adler, John Buckley, Sam Landol, Tom Rarich, Dave Rasmussen, and Rita Yavinski. As a result of our 1990 project to determine the criteria for successful alliances, I began to incorporate practices in my own work that led to many successful alliances.

Thanks also to Rosemary O'Mahony and Mike Bass at Andersen Consulting for their support and insight. They have championed the alliance cause with me for many years. And thanks to Steve Elliot for his support, which enabled me to write this book.

Special acknowledgment and thanks to my coauthor Melissa Giovagnoli, who convinced me to take on this project with her, and whose questioning and prodding enabled me to clearly define what it takes to develop and manage alliances.

Most of all I want to thank my wife, Kathleen, and our children, Robert, Donna, and Michael; their support and understanding allowed me to undertake writing this book.

Chicago, Illinois   John K. Conlon
April 1998

The Authors

Melissa Giovagnoli is the author of four successful books, including *Make Your Connections Count: The Six-Step System to Build Your MegaNetwork* (Dearborn). For more than sixteen years she has been helping individuals and corporations understand the powerful networking process she created that accelerates growth through alliance strategies. In this age where the network is quickly becoming the dominant form of organizational development, Giovagnoli offers a unique and effective system for achieving twenty-first century growth. Her community alliance-building program has been used by organizations such as AT&T.

Giovagnoli has also been a guest on both radio and television, including on *The Today Show*, CNN, WGN, CNBC, and Fox. Her most recent book was featured on Oprah Winfrey's program. Her clients have included Dean Foods, AT&T, Humana Hospitals, and Price Waterhouse, as well as dozens of smaller companies and organizations. She is president of Service Showcase, Inc., an innovative training, strategic planning, and consulting firm.

John K. Conlon is a director of alliances at Andersen Consulting. He is a leading proponent of alliances as part of corporate business strategies; for fourteen years he has worked with senior executives to develop and implement alliance strategies. He advises major corporations and small companies on implementing alliances to expand their markets, and is a leader in working with competing companies that want to form alliances to meet their business goals.

Conlon provides thought leadership on alliance development and management, and he regularly addresses senior managers on the topic. His experience has enabled him to develop valuable tools, rules of thumb, and methods.

He earned a bachelor of science degree in electrical engineering from the University of Notre Dame. He lives in Wheaton, Illinois, with his wife Kathleen and their three children, Robert, Donna, and Michael. Since 1987, he has volunteered as a leader in the Boy Scouts of America.

The Power of Two

Introduction

The Power of Two Alliances

It was almost three years ago when Melissa and I met to discuss our potential alliance opportunity: this book. It started as a mutual colleague's suggestion that Melissa—a specialist in using networking as an organizational growth model—contact me because, as she put it, "I heard John speak, and I think you two share the same perspective on alliances."

From that original meeting we both discovered that we not only share the same perspective, we possess remarkably similar visions and values. We were pleased to learn that we both subscribe to the belief that the foundation of any good alliance is a warm personal relationship rather than some cold piece of paper. We both saw that the success of companies moving forward into the next century depends on their commitment to focusing on relationships rather than transactions. We both agreed that two alliance-minded people, each representing a different organization, could orchestrate opportunity-driven collaborations that would be far more effective than the deal-making partnerships of the past. We coined the term "Power of Two" to describe our concept and began working and writing together. Those efforts resulted in this book.

With Melissa's extensive work with networks and mine as a director of alliances at Andersen Consulting, we found ourselves wonderfully positioned to provide a guide for forming a new type of alliance. Through our many real-life experiences and extensive research into hundreds of different alliances, we sat down to write a book that would offer a road map to achieving collaborative effectiveness. As you will see, this book is very user friendly. We didn't want to write something academic or theoretical. We wanted something that would offer readers tools and techniques for forming and managing a new business alliance in a new business environment.

To that end, each chapter is filled with ideas and questions designed to help you do all of the following:

- Choose the right person to head up your alliance efforts.
- Create a strategy that will allow you to partner productively with competitors, smaller and larger companies, and organizations with dissimilar cultures.
- Build speed and flexibility into the alliance by building trusting relationships.
- Pursue opportunities through knowledge and idea exchanges.
- Manage the alliance so that conflicts and concerns (the kind that routinely tear apart traditional collaborations) don't undermine a productive partnership.
- Develop an alliance network that you can leverage for all sorts of opportunities.

We don't believe this type of alliance development and management is optional; it is a necessity of a business era where teaming and relationships are becoming far more important than deal making and power brokering. Both Melissa and I have seen more than one organization fail in partnering efforts because they were stuck in the old partnering paradigm. Just as importantly, we've seen a number of companies cocreate great new opportunities because they embraced the Power of Two concept.

Throughout this book we'll help you transition from old to new partnering approaches. One of the best ways to start making this shift is by developing a Power of Two mind-set. It is a mind-set that is open, adaptable, proactive, innovative, and informed. Most of us think that we and our organizations possess this mind-set when we set forth to team with other companies. To test whether you do, answer the following questions:

1. Do you know who's partnering with whom in your industry? Are you aware of all the alliances being formed? Have you analyzed which companies might make good partners for your organization?

2. Have you ruled out organizations as potential partners because they're too small or too large, because they're competitors, or because they have different cultures than yours?

3. Have you identified people within your own organization who are great collaborators, who possess the communication and relationship-building skills critical for partnering, who have built strong networks internally as well as externally?

4. Are you open to investing in an alliance that promises no immediate return on your investment? Are you willing to make your initial goal acquiring exciting new ideas and information?

5. Have you ever trusted a collaborator enough that you were willing to work with them without a formal contract? Would you be willing to do so in the future?

6. If you formed an alliance to pursue one opportunity and another one popped up unexpectedly, would you be willing to switch directions if the former was a "sure thing" and the latter wasn't but held greater promise?

7. How much do you know about a prospective partner's culture, about its philosophies, policies, and procedures? Do you have a sense of its beliefs and values?

A Case Study

The Power of Two alliance concept, like many alliance approaches, isn't worth much unless it's grounded in example and practical advice. We hope to provide you with plenty of both. We'll try and answer the most commonly asked questions and address the issues that often come up when people are interested in forming and managing this new type of alliance.

To give you a sense of how we'll do this, we'd like to share with you a hypothetical case study where we've inserted in parentheses the representative chapter related to the issue being discussed. This should preview some of the topics we cover and facilitate understanding of how our ideas fit into a typical alliance development process.

ABC Technologies, Inc., a company that designs and develops alternative fuel systems for a number of vehicles for Fortune 500 Car Company, Inc., created an alliance with Fortune 500 approximately two years ago. It began when ABC's director of marketing, Susan Wield, met John Janson, the director of marketing for Fortune 500 Car, at a trade show in Chicago. John and Susan spoke extensively about their business connection. As they spoke, they also shared their mutual interest in capitalizing on the relationships they'd developed at a number of industry organizations in order to pursue various opportunities, including building alternative fuel vehicles (Chapter Four: Leveraged Network). Susan teased John that she thought it would be highly unlikely that the two companies could actually become alliance partners, but John, who was always eager to explore exciting if unlikely possibilities, decided to analyze some scenarios (Chapter Five: The Alliance Champion).

John started talking with his company's director of operations and director of finance separately, asking questions like, "What if we formed an alliance with a company that could cocreate an opportunity like developing new fuel delivery systems?" To his surprise John found his colleagues rather receptive. Each suggested taking the idea forward to their annual strategic planning session, which was coming up within the next month. John brought the positive news back to Susan during their biweekly phone calls to one another. With John's enthusiastic support of the idea, Susan decided to shop it around in her own organization.

After speaking with several people, Susan met with ABC's head of research and development, Adam Sampson. Adam said he was taking a class in his MBA curriculum that focused on strategic alliances. He mentioned to Susan that he thought their organization would also be very supportive. He said there were constant rumors that the company would have fewer dollars in upcoming years to support the kind of R&D Adam thought necessary to sustain its current profit level. An alliance such as the one Susan had in mind might open new, more profitable markets to the company.

Susan took this information back to John, who then passed it on to his growing network of alliance supporters. John and Susan continued to discuss their initiative and to strategize how to proceed in building a successful alliance (Chapter Six: Alliance Analysis). Their discussion included many questions: Who would make decisions related to the alliance (Chapter Eight: Rules of Engagement)? How would they avoid the suspicion and second-guessing that they experienced in past partnerships (Chapter Nine: Trust)? How, given the companies' very different cultures, might they deal with those differences so that one partner wouldn't get disgusted with the other's way of doing things (Chapter Ten: Cultural Criteria)?

When the two organizations and their champions (Susan and John) met they spent the majority of their three hours together discussing the alternative fuel car market and other ideas and possibilities that dovetailed with their combined strengths (Chapter Seven: Cocreating Business Opportunities). This included ideas such as cross-licensing the use of the new technology they codevelop, cocreating new technologies with additional alliance partners, and sharing ongoing research findings.

Avoiding the Mistakes That Doom Alliances

One of the catalysts for this book was our observation of and participation in alliances that failed. As much as we hope you'll adopt our Power of Two strategy, we also hope you'll reject the myths, misconceptions, and myopia that plague collaborative efforts. See if any of the following mistakes sound familiar:

Putting the wrong people in charge of the alliance. In Power of Two alliances, champions are brilliant at building relationships, establishing trust, and achieving consensus. We've seen many alliance heads and relationship managers who were lone rangers, inflexible and unwilling to compromise. Their reasoning was: we need to put a strong guy in charge of our alliance work to balance out their strong guy. If "strong guy" means obstinate and individualistic, the alliance is in trouble.

Not taking alliances seriously. In other words, some senior managers don't support the alliance as much as tolerate it. They don't provide it with the necessary resources, and top executives don't communicate the importance of alliances to the company's business strategy. Power of Two companies recognize that alliances are their future and approach them with great seriousness. One of the largest makers of computer networking equipment has shifted from growing through mergers and acquisitions to growth through alliances. Like many organizations that are moving toward this new form of growth, this manufacturer is now developing support of its alliance partners by switching numerous engineers and customer service resources to that area. It has made financial, strategic, and people commitments to alliances, and those commitments are felt both within the company and at partnering organizations.

Suspecting one's partner of hidden motives. When two organizations partner, there's always room for suspicion and jealousy. Invariably someone in Organization A will say, "Organization B is getting a lot more out of our partnership than we are." When you work with a partner for the first time, a certain amount of questioning should be expected. Problems occur when the questioning escalates to animosity, charges, and countercharges. Power of Two alliances stop this escalation by building a trusting relationship between alliance champions and making sure a plan is in place to address questions from alliance partners.

Winging it. Too many alliances move forward on a wing and a prayer. A company that would never operate without a detailed business plan thinks nothing of partnering without having ever mapped out an alliance strategy. If you don't take alliances seriously, winging it is a frequent sin.

Partnering prosaically. In other words, there's no poetry in the collaboration, no creativity, no inspiration. In traditional deal-making alliances, companies get together because they need each other to accomplish a clear short-term goal—for example, to sell a computer system when one company has the technical expertise and the other has the customer contacts. Such short-term, obvious opportunities are in short supply. To find opportunities today, alliances have to dig, to be imaginative.

Not being alliance-ready. Some organizations simply aren't prepared to partner. They don't have the vaguest idea how to collaborate with a competitor, how to structure motivating compensation for the sales force selling alliance products and services, or even whether a prospective partner has the same alliance goals as they do. According to a recent report published by Andersen Consulting, most financial services companies are betting much of their corporate future on forming and managing strategic alliances. The average U.S. bank, for example, had thirty alliances at the time the report was compiled, up from twelve a year earlier. Indeed, more alliances in this industry were formed in the six months before the report was compiled than in the six years before that. When polled, many of the financial services executives stated that they expected to enter into fifty or more alliances in the succeeding three years, which they anticipated would account for as much as 50 percent of their revenues. Yet the most revealing findings discovered by the study show that the majority of institutions are extremely unprepared to handle the challenges of alliance development.

Not knowing when to end an alliance. Some last far longer than they should. Companies partner, have some success, and continue collaborating out of misspent loyalty or sheer inertia. This is an age of rapidly shifting alliances, of moving quickly from one partner to the next as need and opportunity dictate. Power of Two allies recognize that their alliance is temporary; they'll work together awhile, find other partners for other goals, and then repartner somewhere down the road.

Learning from the Experiences of Others

Wherever possible in this book we use examples of real businesses that have either failed or succeeded in their alliance-building efforts. Some of our case histories are drawn from our involvement with organizations as consultants. Others we were only involved with peripherally or heard about from various other sources. In some instances we've created hypothetical and composite scenarios based on our experiences to illustrate points. Though we sometimes name the organizations in our examples, we often have to use fictitious names because of confidentiality agreements and other reasons.

The point is that this book is based on the alliance-building and management efforts of a wide variety of organizations. Through our combined experience as consultants, we've worked with a wide variety of alliances, including big companies with other big companies, big companies with small companies, mid-sized companies partnering in a joint venture, a vendor collaborating with its customer, and competitors deciding to create an alliance to pursue an opportunity. We've counseled companies on how to analyze and choose partners for an alliance, how to select alliance champions, how to maintain trust between partners, and how to cocreate alliance opportunities. We've seen just about everything that can happen when two companies try to join forces, and we've encountered just about every type of obstacle to a productive alliance. We've translated the lessons learned into this book.

A Guide to More Powerful Alliances

We've observed an emerging trend that makes us think that this book will do a real service for organizations attempting to form and maintain alliances. Specifically, more companies than ever before want to team with other companies, but more than ever before are dissatisfied with the results of their collaborations. The problem is that no one teaches us how to partner in MBA programs or on the job; it's a competency that most companies lack. To partner the old way—to acquire another organization or "do a deal"—required more financial acumen than partnering skills. It was simply a matter of making sure all the numbers checked out.

Alliances today are more complex and varied in scope and purpose than those in the past. It takes a certain amount of knowledge and a process to make them work. That's what we hope to provide in the following pages. From analyzing whether a prospective ally is right for your organization (and if you're right for it) to setting forth rules of engagement that will keep the alliance running smoothly, we'll offer a variety of helpful ideas and hints. We'll also define the Power of Two process that will give you a framework for executing your alliance efforts—a framework that fits with the emerging business environment.

We're entering the age of the alliance. From organizations embracing teams to companies partnering with competitors, we're seeing a radical shift in how business is conducted throughout the world. Alliances are rapidly becoming a critical part of every company's strategic growth initiative.

Who will the big winners be in the upcoming years? The organizations with the best alliance skills would be our biased answer. But our bias has a basis in fact. Organization after organization emphasize networking and relationship-building skills. They're setting up training programs in these areas, creating relationship manager positions, and encouraging their people to leverage their business networks like never before. These are great first steps for building the alliance infrastructure that is a Power of Two necessity. The fact that companies have taken these steps indicates that they recognize the need to approach alliance building aggressively and from fresh angles.

As noted by Jocelyn Carter-Miller, vice president and director of Latin American and Caribbean operations for Motorola, "If you haven't realized it yet, we are in a new world of work. This means that the rules that applied even last year won't apply next year. We all need to understand the power of networking and relationship building." In a recent interview, Carter-Miller spoke of a very successful alliance with a Latin American company that had been a distributor of Motorola products for forty years previously. She said that the alliance's great success was due to the strong relationship she established with the distribution company's president. Indeed, Motorola held a minority position in the operation of a paging network. The venture, which lasted four years, was so successful that it acquired 33 percent of the Argentinean paging market by 1997, ending in a very profitable sale for both partners. When the alliance was in full swing, Carter-Miller found total trust and respect between herself and her alliance partner. "If you removed all the other rules of building alliances but forming strong relationships," she said, "I believe, in this case, we could still have built a successful initiative."

Though we don't recommend forgetting all the other rules of alliance building, Carter-Miller's experiences do echo our own and many of those with whom we have worked. The Power of Two finds its energy source in trusting relationships between two representatives of partnering organizations. When you have two alliance champions in place who have established a bond of trust, you've established the single most important relationship for the alliance's success.

This book will help you choose the champion who can forge a strong, trusting relationship with another champion. It will also give your champion and your organization a process for turning that relationship into a Power of Two alliance.

Chapter One

The Magic Number

When we refer to the Power of Two, we're referring to a distinct form of alliance. In the following pages we define it, differentiate it, and demonstrate why it's uniquely effective for opportunity-seeking organizations. First, though, we want you to think about the "alliance impulse."

Since the modern organization was created, the organizational instinct has been to view alliances as vehicles to become bigger than and more dominant over competitors. Mergers and acquisitions have been the major form of this activity. In the past decade we've seen a great deal of partnering with vendors designed to give companies competitive advantage. We've also witnessed many "alliances of convenience"—partnerships between companies designed to capitalize on specific, time-sensitive opportunities.

For the moment, let's define alliances in the broadest terms possible: a temporary or permanent joining of two organizations through force or mutual agreement. Given this, here are four common reasons for alliances to be formed:

- To become larger and dominate a market
- To acquire expertise, technology, money, or other resources the organization lacks
- To fend off an aggressive move by a competitor, becoming bigger and stronger and in a better position to deal with that competitor
- To do a deal; to use combined resources to jump on a market bandwagon

In most instances, the alliance impulse is the same as the cata-lyst behind the development of the Roman Empire, the Soviet Union, or the United States' doctrine of Manifest Destiny. Bigger is better. In size there is strength. Companies, like countries, wanted to conquer the world—or at least their corner of the world.

Partnerships, collaborations, alliances, mergers, and acquisitions all came about because organizations were obsessed with the over-arching goal of bigness. Unfortunately, that impulse lingers even though the business environment has changed.

A New Environment, a New Type of Alliance

The following four factors have emerged to render traditional al-liances obsolete:

- The need to move fast and in any direction
- The rapid pace of technological advance
- The need to find viable solutions to growing and increasingly complex problems
- The interconnectedness of the world

Let's examine each of these factors and consider their impact on alliances.

The Need to Move Fast and in Any Direction

Organizations may not be a dollar short, but they are increasingly a day late. Talk to most company CEOs and they'll tell you that it takes too damn long to develop a new product, discover and target an emerging market, and put a new process in place. It's as if we've been moving in slow motion for years and now everything has been speeded up to a comically hyper pace (though no one's laughing). Consequently, companies in traditional alliances feel as if they can never do anything quickly enough—they're always at least one step behind because of their size and bureaucracy.

For instance, advertising agencies have been scrambling to find partners to build web sites for their clients. They know this is a hot area experiencing explosive growth and they want to get in on it. Lacking the internal expertise to provide this service for their clients, they're searching high and low for outside partners. The problem is they're forming alliances of convenience. In other words, it suits the agency's purpose to ally itself with a web site designer. It's a pure transactional relationship that's formed on the spur of the moment; little thought is given to relationships between key people, to a meshing of cultures and philosophies.

Certainly these ad agency–web site provider collaborations may give the agency's clients what they want today and earn both partners some money. But what happens when a shift in the market occurs? Then the client says, "Our site is costing us a ton of money and we're not getting a return on our investment. We see a lot more potential in an Intranet site, one that we can use as a learning and training tool for all our employees. You should have given us help on this, and if you can't do something for us right now that works, we're going to look elsewhere."

The partnership is taken aback. The agency blames the web site designer and the designer blames the agency. They try to provide an Intranet site, but they don't have much experience in this area and the client again threatens to take its business elsewhere. Because the relationship between the agency and site designer is purely transactional, there's great animosity between them. They can't work together to smoothly and quickly shift gears and move in the desired direction. They pull apart, fighting each other's ideas, and they eventually lose the business.

Organizations need to rethink the entire concept of speed. In the past it was said that being "the first with the most" would lead to dominance in a product category. Now you can be the first with the most, but before you can dominate, the market has shifted under your feet and you have to be first in a different way. Speed is no longer about rushing into markets. It's about darting this way and that, being able to move quickly in anticipation of where trends or technologies will lead the market.

Consider three things that slow down a traditional partnership:

- *Legal issues.* The contractual agreement between the two partners doesn't cover all contingencies, and when the x factor is introduced (which always happens these days) precious time is lost as the two groups attempt to revise the contract or debate who should do what.

- *Suspicion.* Why is Partner A so eager to shift the alliance's focus from Europe to Asia? Why is Partner B so unwilling to bring its considerable expertise to bear on the problem? Question after question about the other partner causes each to say, "Whoa, we better slow down here."

- *Too many decision makers.* Too many people need to be consulted before a move can be made. There are multiple linkages between the two joined organizations, and the typical process is to get key people to sign off on a decision before it can be made. Invariably at least one of these people puts a kibosh on the idea or delays it in some way.

The Rapid Pace of Technological Advance

Technology is the second environmental element mandating a new type of alliance. Let's look at an obvious factor first, then a more subtle one.

Just about every industry is experiencing what we call *technology vertigo*: a dizzying whirl of technological possibilities, each with the potential to revolutionize processes and products. The old management mind-set views this and thinks, "Who can I partner with to give me the best chance of capitalizing on the hot new technology?" Not too many years ago, when the pace of technological change was significantly slower, this might have been appropriate. Now it's an attempt to find a quick and easy solution to a complex problem. It equates partner with panacea, assuming that the solution now and forever is to find exactly the right company with exactly the right technology.

Do you partner with Company A that seems to have the cutting-edge product available today or with Company B that seems like it will take the cutting edge to a higher level tomorrow? One technology will speed up production but also presents training problems. Another technology people learn to master quickly but production gains aren't as great. With all the conundrums and trade-offs that technological vertigo begets, there's rarely one clear choice for any organization.

We've worked with banks who have a number of potential partners in place to deal with electronic banking. They look out and see their customers being enticed by nontraditional competitors such as computer hardware and software companies, Internet organizations, and service bureaus. What electronic banking technology will most appeal to the bank's customers? The answer depends on many unresolved service and price issues. These banks are intelligently saying to themselves: we don't know what's going to happen, so let's give ourselves a number of partnering options that cover a range of scenarios.

There's also a more subtle driver of alliance redefinition. Technology has made it possible to exchange information faster and better than ever before. From e-mail to Intranet and Extranet sites, information transfer tools abound. On the plus side, it means partners can reach joint decisions faster (theoretically, at least) because both have virtually instant access to the same information. Not only that, but the new technology makes it possible to tailor information to meet an alliance's specific needs, categorizing key topics and making it easy to access the data required.

From a traditional alliance perspective, however, there's a negative side to these developments. Companies are still guarding certain pieces of data; they still are reluctant to let outsiders see financial data, strategic plans, or market research. But without a free and easy exchange of information between allies, resentment builds. The complaint "I'm being kept out of the loop" is one we've heard often. Traditional alliances aren't set up for electronic information transfer; the trust that allows it isn't there.

The Need for Viable Solutions to Growing, Increasingly Complex Problems

The third driver of alliance redefinition is the sheer magnitude of the problems facing organizations. You can no longer just throw money at problems and expect them to go away. Learning how to compete globally or dealing with simmering environmental issues bedevil many organizations. Increasingly sophisticated customers demand better and more innovative service from their companies.

To deal with these difficult problems, companies need to pool their resources and find the best possible way of applying their collective knowledge to search for a solution. Traditional alliances tend to share certain resources only in certain situations: there's all sorts of red tape and restrictions attached to finding solutions. You hear "this is how we do it at Company A" or complaints about culture clashes.

In addition, company after company has found that it needs help to solve a customer's problems or capitalize on its opportunities. Yet if you look at companies that have come together for this purpose, you see a tendency to compete with each other to solve the customer's problem. Each has organizational agendas that dictate how it helps the customer. For instance, Company A wants the alliance to be successful so it will receive more business from the customer; Company B's president is interested in the prestige attached to working with the customer; Company C will stay in the alliance only if it calls the shots when working for this particular customer.

The Interconnectedness of the World

Companies used to be like John Wayne characters: rugged individualists proud of their independence. Back then, alliances of any type were usually avoided. Relatively recently, however, organizations recognized that they couldn't go it alone, that in a global, rapidly changing world they lacked in-house some of the resources and expertise they needed. So they merged, acquired, outsourced, and formed partnerships to obtain what they needed. They moved from independence to dependence.

Now we're seeing a second shift to interdependence. Instead of one company relying on another to conquer a market, one company's fate is linked to countless other organizations. It means you can't simply form one alliance and be done with it.

Merged organizations, companies that partner with one particular vendor, and those that come together to "do deals" are especially vulnerable to this environmental shift. They lock themselves into exclusive relationships, shutting themselves out of the networks required to function effectively in an interdependent world. Organizational networking permits companies to shuffle partners as opportunities dictate; it plugs them into a network not only of deal making but of information and ideas.

No one, two, three, four, or five companies together have the expertise, creativity, contacts, experience, money, technology, and other resources necessary to capitalize on rapidly changing opportunities. One day an opportunity may emerge in Romania; another day it may have its roots in a new process pioneered by a consultant in Iowa. It's impossible to know in advance who your perfect partner for that opportunity will be; things are changing too fast to tie your fate to one partner. Only if you're part of a broad-based, flexible network can you find the partner you need when you need it.

Traditional alliances are ill-suited to deal with the environmental factors just described. To understand the problems they encounter, let's look at the common structures of traditional alliances:

- One company acquires another.
- One company merges with another.
- One company partners with another (often with a vendor-supplier).
- One company collaborates with another for a specific purpose (to develop a new technology, to go global, or the like).

More important than the structure, however, are the traits that define these relationships. Traditional alliances usually exhibit most of these traits:

- The goal is short-term profit, so long-term planning is the exception rather than the rule.
- A master-slave relationship exists between allies of different sizes, such that the bigger partner dominates the smaller.
- Many different people manage the alliance; a bureaucracy governs decision making.
- The alliance is an island in a sea of other alliances; it exists apart, avoiding communication with other groups.
- The alliance becomes focused and driven by one particular objective; the participants have trouble shifting away from that objective as market conditions shift.
- Little synergy exists. In mergers or acquisitions one company is subsumed by the other; in collaborations or partnerships two companies coexist but don't freely share people, ideas, and information.

As a result, problems arise between partners: lack of trust, poor communication, absence of defining personal relationships, no commitment beyond short-term financial gain, culture clashes, impatience, inequality such that one partner dictates terms to the other, the involvement of many people in the alliance but little real management of it, reactivity rather than proactivity, and a lack of imagination because each partner wants to keep great new ideas to itself rather than share them.

You can boil down these and other problems until you're left with a single, inescapable malady: organizations form and manage alliances as if there were only one organization involved.

Or, to put a finer point on it, *they fail to take advantage of the Power of Two*.

The Power of Two Alliance

The "two" in Power of Two refers to the spirit as much as the structure of the alliance. It suggests a bond between two entities, a bond cemented by trust, communication, commitment, and sharing. Unlike traditional alliances, the partnership is equal and synergistic. The power derives from the integration of two equals.

Let's define Power of Two in less esoteric terms. Perhaps the best way is to list and describe the eight traits that are part of every Power of Two alliance.

1. Alliance Champions

Alliance champions are visionaries and strategists. Each ally has one, and the alliance relationship rises (or falls) based on their relationship. They're acutely aware of where management wants the organization to be in five years, and they're searching for relationships that will help them get there. Alliance champions perceive the gaps between what organizations have and what they need to achieve long-term goals; they're skilled at filling those gaps by making alliances.

All of which doesn't mean that champions are pie-in-the-sky dreamers. Along with their vision, they have a strong strain of practicality. Most Power of Two relationships don't form overnight. They need to be nurtured, and champions are great nurturers. They aren't discouraged when alliances don't provide an expected return. In fact, they are skilled at working toward small victories to overcome objections and other barriers to alliances.

Champions are skilled at working across boundaries. They don't rule out companies as partners because they're competitors or because they're too small or large. They're also skilled at working across internal boundaries. Champions are well connected throughout their organizations and have access to a range of resources denied to others.

"Relationship manager" is a job title that is popping up with increasing frequency, and we need to differentiate this role from that of champions. Organizations have created this position because they see the need for one person to coordinate the various relationships they're forming with other companies. Typical relationship managers have sales or marketing backgrounds; that perspective informs the way they manage, because they will likely measure relationship success by whether it generates results (meaning income) in the first twelve months.

There are many relationship managers out there, if not in name then in deed. They are short-term thinkers who spend most of their time setting up meetings, going to various functions and "working the room," and writing reports about all the relationships they've made and managed.

Relationship managers tend to be impatient deal makers; they're the manic-depressives of the business world, high when they do a deal and low when a deal falls through. They have difficulty waiting for a relationship to evolve or bouncing back from defeat. Alliance champions, however, are patient, persistent, and resilient. They accept that some Power of Two alliances will take time to come together, that it could be years before the interests of the two partners converge with slowly emerging markets.

2. Infrastructure Network

Perhaps the best way to describe this trait is by reference to a company that has made the transition to this networking approach. For years IBM was the rugged individualist of American corporations; alliances were a cultural taboo. Over time, however, IBM senior management recognized that, big and powerful as IBM was, it couldn't go it alone; in a global marketplace with ever-shifting markets and trends it was more handicap than advantage to rely only on its own resources. So management developed a partnering culture, actively seeking out other companies (from competitors to smaller entrepreneurs) as allies. IBM rewards its people who work with business partners to deliver value to their mutual customers. It recognizes that the only way to deliver a networked world to customers is to be networked itself.

Infrastructure networks are more than just knowing lots of people in lots of companies. It's easy to mistake activity for accomplishment. Power of Two allies are linked on a deeper level than just knowing one another and talking about working together. The infrastructure network is bound together by a common strategy and vision. Power of Two companies have sat down together, exchanged knowledge, analyzed markets, and created a long-term plan. Perhaps the plan includes what type of opportunities to pursue together. There's a mutual understanding of each other's culture and how they can blend together to make a strategy happen.

An infrastructure network gives Power of Two allies astonishing reach. It's not the mere presence of numerous partners throughout the world that is the differentiator. It's the depth and strength of the bond between all the allies in the network that make it unique.

People sometimes become confused when we talk about the Power of Two and a Network of Many. For now you should understand that although an alliance is a one-on-one relationship it exists within a larger universe of prospective Power of Two alliances. It encourages forming new one-on-one relationships as situations change.

3. A *Variety of Partner Possibilities*

In traditional alliances there are unwritten rules about who is and isn't an appropriate partner. Partnering with competitors is forbidden; allying oneself with a vendor who also works with a competitor is also taboo. Big companies can only acquire small companies; equal partnerships between the two are impossible. Traditional allies often have compatible cultures; it's unlikely that a hip, informal start-up would partner with a hundred-year-old market leader.

In Power of Two alliances, every organization is a potential partner regardless of size, culture, or competitive status. Let's discuss this
last qualifier by way of an example:

A number of companies in the computer industry received a request
for a proposal from a state governmental organization. It wanted
help in building an information system that would capture information from tax forms and monitor compliance with tax regulations.
Two of the companies—let's call them Computer Company and
Consulting Company—had service groups that competed against
each other in the past. Both had alliance champions who recognized
the benefits of working together. Consulting Company had the business and project management skills required by the governmental
group, and Computer Company had the product and technological
expertise needed. In addition, the champions at both recognized
that this alliance had much greater potential than ones with their
traditional, noncompetitive partners. Best of all, there might be all
sorts of significant future benefits from this alliance, such as delivering the solution to the other forty-nine states.

At the same time, the champions recognized the reality of the
situation: competition between the two companies in the past had
been fierce. To make the alliance happen, both champions devised
a number of win-win scenarios. One of them came into use at a critical meeting when the tension between a few key executives from
each company became palpable. The champion from Computer
Company spoke, admitting that it lacked the project management
competency to design an effective solution to the governmental
agency's problem. Before this meeting, the Computer Company alliance champion had stressed to other executives that they needed
to be straightforward with their prospective ally in order to build
trust. Still, the Computer Company executives were surprised to
hear him admit to competitors that they had shortcomings with respect to this business opportunity. The admission, though, eased
some of the tension in the room and enabled the executives from
Consulting Company to concede that they were missing the neces-

sary technological skills. Both made concessions from a revenue standpoint and focused everyone's attention on the needs of the client and not on their own needs.

Not only did the alliance win the government project, but its members positioned themselves perfectly for a number of other lucrative projects down the road.

4. Internal as Well as External Focus

In many traditional alliances you'll find that the emphasis is on bringing two outside organizations together rather than encouraging internal partnerships. Power of Two alliances are marked by partnering cultures. The external alliance structure is mirrored internally.

AT&T, for instance, is beginning to grasp the possibilities of aligning two divisions, departments, or other groups to focus on a specific goal. As in most organizations, AT&T's various departments have a history of "siloism," in which people move up through the ranks vertically and there's little horizontal integration. Now, however, they're becoming proficient at creating internal alliances with the help of alliance champions and other Power of Two tools. The WorldNet group, for instance, was created to provide Internet access for AT&T customers. Tension existed between WorldNet people and those who sell local services; the latter were so focused on local sales that they didn't see the benefit of WorldNet to their efforts. Alliance champions, however, brought the two groups together by demonstrating the cost savings and sales possibilities of an internal partnership.

5. Trust

Trust doesn't just have touchy-feely benefits; it's a great marketing tool for alliance partners. We've found that there's a synergistic build-up of cross-promotional support that flows from trust. Power of Two partners are proud of each other. They're not afraid to refer their allies to customers or other companies; they trust them sufficiently that they know they're working hard to do a good job. As a result of this trust, people naturally volunteer their allies' names. They don't have to be pushed to do so and they don't supply their names with the caveat, "Well, they're our partners in this venture, but you have to watch them closely because. . . ." The trust is unequivocal, as is the recommendation.

Trust is what makes it possible for allies—and sometimes competitors—to exchange sensitive information and other assets that have been traditionally regarded as proprietary. In the health care industry, pharmaceutical companies such as Baxter and Abbott continue to form alliances with smaller, innovative biotech companies, exchanging research and development capabilities for large, developed-market distribution channels. One learns new distribution tricks while the other gains R&D ideas.

6. Speed

Power of Two alliances can move faster because they're relationship-based and are run by empowered champions. There are no delays because of petty bickering and jealousy over who does what and gets what. The trust that has been built accelerates decision making—no one holds up an important initiative because of boundary disputes or political maneuvering. When an opportunity surfaces, the champions have the freedom to move quickly and seize it.

7. Flexibility

Many companies that collaborate are more rigid when joined than when apart. One organization's policies and procedures are layered on the other's rules and regulations, and together they have almost no room to maneuver. Company Y's policy is to avoid certain markets because it has had no success in them; Company Z only pursues opportunities that fit its demographic and psychographic requirements. A Power of Two alliance has rules, but they're rules of engagement—policies designed for how the alliance will be managed.

In other words, they're rules for future growth rather than past policy. In one sense, forming a Power of Two alliance is like creating a new entity. It is not bound by tradition or burdened by past successes or failures. It has the freedom to grow and take whatever shape makes sense.

8. Innovation

Imagine being freed from the imperative of making a quick buck. Or having to compete with the same products and services against a crowded field of competitors. Or wasting enormous amounts of time and energy just keeping the alliance together. Power of Two alliances free people from these restrictions. Just as important, they provide them with fresh knowledge. Too often, traditional partners are wary of exchanging "classified" information. Power of Two alliances give partners access to fresh data, which in turn stimulates fresh ways of thinking. They encourage continual and open communication in the belief that the better the information, the better the ideas. Here's an example:

> Church's Chicken and White Castle Systems have formed an innovative Power of Two alliance. According to their collaborative agreement, White Castle will operate Church's Chicken restaurants from within its own restaurants, allowing Church's to gain access to nontraditional locations, and both companies will leverage each other's customer base. Church's is strong during dinner hours; White Castle has a strong lunch-time market. Though this alliance makes perfect sense, it also might cause a traditional business executive to lose his lunch. These competitors take a big-picture view of their relationship, and that gives them the ability to be highly innovative.

The Other Difference

The biggest difference between traditional alliances and Power of Two alliances has to do with ultimate goals. The former are created to capitalize on an opportunity that exists. The latter are established to capitalize on an opportunity that will emerge. In the fast-moving, rapidly changing world we now live in, organizations need to position themselves for trends, technologies, and markets that haven't fully emerged; they may only be possibilities when the Power of Two alliance is formed.

The key is to be ready to move when opportunities present themselves. Traditional alliances jump into a market when it's hot. In the past this was fine; markets stayed hot for a while and competitors were relatively slow to react. Today the process is accelerated. By the time the alliance is created and starts moving, it's too late.

Anticipation, preparation, proactive planning, visioning—these are all attributes of opportunistic Power of Two alliances. Clearly these attributes confer many benefits on companies in the current business environment. The next chapter explores these benefits in detail.

Chapter Two

The Advantages of Joining the Power of Two Movement

Why hasn't everyone started forming Power of Two alliances? Given the fit between marketplace trends and this new type of alliance, you'd think organizations would quickly see the value. Concepts such as alliance champions and infrastructure networks seem to offer obvious benefits.

We've found that the benefits aren't always so obvious. The problem is that a traditional alliance such as a merger or an acquisition provides immediately understandable advantages. A merger would help a company dominate a market; an acquisition might provide a company with a needed technology, product, or service.

The Power of Two alliance doesn't always offer such clear-cut advantages. Sometimes the edge is more subtle. Other times it's long-term. We've also found that positioning yourself for a potential opportunity is not as exciting as pouncing on an existing one. Given intense pressure for improved short-term performance, it's difficult to appreciate that "opportunity positioning" is absolutely essential for future success.

When you've been focused on immediate, measurable benefits for many years it's not easy to shift perspectives and think in broader, more abstract terms. Only when people grasp the impact of the paradigm shift in the business world—a shift away from centralized power and quick profits and toward decentralization and long-term gains—do they start to see how well suited Power of Two alliances are for the current climate. Flexibility and maneuverability are far more important today than in the past.

We'd like to give you a good sense of what Power of Two alliances can mean to your organization both now and in the future. Let's start out with a rather unusual list of advantages:

1. Opportunity-based alternatives
2. A source of challenging, potentially profitable ideas
3. Competitive synergy
4. A dynamic, partnering culture
5. A necessary diversity of relationships

Opportunity-Based Alternatives

Imagine a world so unpredictable that any current strategy will be rendered obsolete in a year, a month, or even a week. On second thought, such a world really doesn't require much imagination. It's the one we live in, though some organizations still believe that they can rely on traditional formulas for success indefinitely. We've seen companies learn the hard way that markets can become saturated faster than anyone thought possible, that technology can swiftly change both the rules and stakes of the game, that global competition can reach into small, neglected markets and have an impact.

Given this unpredictability, it's crucial to have as many options as possible. You never know what resources, contacts, and information will come in handy. No organization, no matter how large, can acquire all these things. Any organization, no matter how small, can build a network that gives it access to many of these things. Companies well prepared for an uncertain future will have a network of Power of Two alliances in place.

Power of Two alliances offer the advantage of opportunity positioning. An infrastructure network gives an organization access to a range of information, markets, technologies, and ideas that would be far beyond their reach otherwise. Strong relationships with multiple partners increase the odds that they'll be ready to capitalize on an opportunity when and wherever it emerges. Consider this case:

A business software company created an infrastructure network that included a software game designer, a catalog company, and a retired marketing consultant (among others). There was no master plan behind this, simply the assumption that the company would need to expand out of its niche at some point if it wanted to continue to grow. That point came in 1996 when its market share declined because of intense competition from other business software firms. The retired marketing consultant dropped by for his monthly meeting with the business software firm and happened to mention how a client of his had experienced extraordinary success with a toy catalog; he also mentioned a study that documented the rising number of software games purchased via direct mail. The company immediately called in its other partners, a new catalog was born, and an opportunity was seized. They had positioned themselves perfectly for an opportunity they didn't know (at the time) would emerge.

You can't do this sort of thing if you maintain the old short-list partner mentality, which dictates that you limit your allies to a precious few, that only companies who meet a set of rigid criteria are allowed to partner with you.

A short list is a bad idea in a big world. What happens when a great opportunity blossoms in Tanzania? What do you do when there's a technological breakthrough that can greatly benefit your customers? How quickly can you implement a dynamic new process? The answers depend on how many relationships you've built. If you only have a few alliances, then the odds are against capitalizing on the Tanzanian opportunity. Building an infrastructure of multiple allies confers competitive advantage in virtually any marketplace. If your ally doesn't have the expertise you need, your ally's ally will. This alliance network will lead you to the partner you require when you require it.

Consider the Internet. A microcosm of the larger business arena, it's a volatile marketplace with vast potential that's greatly impacted upon by technology. As a result, we're seeing partnering taking place at a feverish pitch so that companies can stay (or at least try to stay) one step ahead of what's happening. For example, a few technology providers are creating Power of Two alliances with each of the three major web browser manufacturers. These providers agree to support and integrate each browser into their product sets so they're prepared to move quickly in the direction of the one that emerges triumphant or to meet the needs of different customer segments that prefer one over the other. One of the three browser companies, Lotus, has gone so far as to support Microsoft's and Netscape's browsers, even though they are its main competition. No one knows how the market will shake out, so everyone is keeping as many options open as possible through various alliances.

In another arena, seventeen highly competitive banks have formed alliances with IBM to develop secure banking processes for Internet transactions. Anticipating high-volume transactions at some point in the future, these banks have come together in an infrastructure network knowing that they'll need to reveal sensitive information to competitors. Yet they recognize that this is far more sensible than being caught without a way to secure such transactions when they become common.

The paradox is that the more partners you have the more you need Power of Two relationships. You need that one-on-one bond to cement each and every alliance. We're not recommending that you go out and partner with everyone who crosses your path. Random alliances are as bad as no alliances at all. We do recommend going out and building strong, trusting relationships with other alliance champions before you need to "use" those relationships. This will position you for opportunities that you can't possibly be aware of at the moment. They are opportunities, however, that you'll want to be ready for when they pop out of nowhere.

A Source of Challenging, Potentially Profitable Ideas

Creativity, thinking out of the box, innovation—these traits are increasingly prized by organizations searching for a competitive edge.

Because of downsizing, outsourcing, and other factors, the traits are decreasingly available in-house.

Partnering with other organizations is a great way to produce an influx of fresh, creative thinking. The problem, of course, is that partnering with a company on your short list merely produces more of the same old thinking. If you've worked with one or two organizations for years and ask them to help you solve a problem or capitalize on an opportunity, you may receive good thinking but probably not breakthrough concepts. In most instances you simply know each other too well—relationship boundaries have been in place for so long that no one is willing (or able) to explore new territory.

We've worked with two companies that have partnered on projects for years. When they meet, it's almost a formality. They go through the motions of discussing the subject at hand and dividing up assignments, but as a principal of one of the companies told us, "I know exactly what they're going to suggest in the meeting, and I suspect they know exactly what we're going to say too."

With an ever-expanding network of collaborators, however, there's a continual supply of challenging ideas. With a strong network infrastructure you not only have access to more partners with more ideas, but everyone is willing and able to communicate those ideas. In short-list situations, companies fall into ruts when dealing with their allies. Familiarity causes everyone to be lazy; they fail to explore new approaches because the established relationship is so easy to deal with. Easy, perhaps, but not necessarily as productive as it might be. The long-time partners we referred to have worked together for more than twenty years. Everything about the collaboration had been routinized: meetings between key people were held on the first Tuesday of each month; twice each year the two partners would talk about ways to keep costs down; an annual picnic attended by employees of both companies was held every summer; conversations between one company executive and his vendor contact seemed almost to follow a script, as the same subjects in the same order were always discussed.

The problem is that it's difficult for either partner to shake up this comfortable arrangement and bring in a new and different concept. Such a concept would require additional work and could possibly lead to disagreement and dissension between partners.

In Power of Two alliances, introducing new concepts that lead to debate and possible disagreement is crucial. The pot is always being stirred by various partners in a network. Ideas are exchanged freely. Many times traditional partners hold back their best concepts; they feel they should keep them for themselves. This idea hoarding robs each partner of potentially great new approaches.

Power of Two alliances are based on trust and the sense that the alliance wouldn't have been formed if it weren't mutually beneficial. Alliance champions constantly build trust and reinforce the notion that if you give, you'll get. As a result, great new ideas are passed back and forth routinely.

Competitive Synergy

A number of years ago, a marketing executive for a Fortune 100 company confided to us that if he could choose anyone as his partner it would be his fiercest competitor, because "if we got together with them and exchanged ideas, sparks would fly."

Until recently collaborating with a competitor was viewed as collaborating with the enemy. Power of Two allies, however, recognize that such a collaboration can be extraordinarily beneficial, especially from a "coopportunity" standpoint. In today's fast-moving, rapidly changing marketplace it's difficult for any one company to possess all the resources necessary to capitalize on most opportunities. Two competitors will both miss out if they stubbornly refuse to combine forces for a specific purpose.

Power of Two alliances are designed to help competitors overcome their fears of collaboration. The solid relationship between alliance champions, the strong foundation of trust, and open and regular communication gives competitors the confidence to work together when the circumstances are right. A dynamic exists between competitors that exists with no other partner. It's a dynamic characterized by two overlapping but distinct perspectives on the same market. When those two perspectives are mixed, new ideas fly. The intensity of this collaboration combined with the knowledge exchanged catalyzes insight, innovation, and the ability to capitalize on opportunities.

AT&T and MCI, for example, are collaborating on a number of fronts, from sharing the use of existing networks to lobbying for new telecommunications legislation. In fact, MCI is also selling excess capacity on AT&T's nationwide wireless system. Although there are numerous benefits from this alliance, a critical one is the ability to offer customers more products and services. Without a partnership it would cost AT&T and MCI far more to create these products and services from scratch. Sharing information, technology, and other resources helps each company better meet customer needs.

Sometimes a Power of Two alliance between competitors provides both partners with exactly what they need when they need it. In 1996 IBM and Storage Tek formed an alliance that allowed IBM to market Storage Tek's disk storage systems. Both companies were in the business, competing in the same markets. But IBM's high-end storage system was delayed in development, and its customers were clamoring for the advanced technology Storage Tek possessed. Storage Tek was strapped for cash, and its R&D efforts to develop new products could go forward quickly with funding from IBM. It was a classic alliance to meet the needs of an existing market.

The potential benefits of competitive synergy can often overcome years of distrust and dislike. Microsoft and Apple Computer have been bitter enemies for years. In fact, Apple sued Microsoft for stealing its user-friendly concept and incorporating it into the Windows operating system. Despite their historical animosity, the two companies discussed the possibility of technology exchanges. Microsoft recognized that Apple has a loyal and significant customer base and that with Apple's help it could market products to that base effectively. Apple's leadership understands that its survival is tied in part to the software company that dominates the market. Internecine warfare is mutually destructive fighting, and emotion fuels it; only logic can create a cease-fire and move the two companies toward an alliance.

Before moving on to the next advantage, we should issue a few words of warning about taking shortcuts to achieve this competitive synergy. Rather than opt for a Power of Two alliance, some companies attempt to hire key people from a competitor, assuming that they can "internalize" their core competency. It rarely works. Consider what happened to Digital Equipment. When in the early 1980s it decided to shift its marketing focus away from manufacturing and engineering customers and toward corporate and business division executives, it looked to IBM, its competitor at the time. But it didn't look at IBM as an alliance partner. Instead, it hired dozens of IBM sales executives for top dollar to implement the new strategy. There were several negative repercussions:

- Former IBM sales managers didn't work well within the "foreign" Digital matrix organization.
- The new salespeople complained that Digital didn't provide them with the same resources and support that they had at IBM.
- Veteran Digital employees didn't work well with the ex-IBM people, resenting their attitudes and their high salaries.

The point of all this is that you can't take a shortcut around Power of Two alliances if you want to achieve a competitive advantage.

Building a Partnering Culture

Many organizations are ill-prepared for the alliance age. Not only do they lack the internal structures that facilitate alliance building but their attitudes are all wrong; they are not thinking in Power of Two terms—of alliance champions, network infrastructures, and information exchanges. They still labor as individuals or as members of departments and divisions; they still attempt to meet individual performance goals; they still view their work in teams as secondary to their work as an employee in Department X.

The companies that partner best with outsiders partner best with insiders. We've found that companies that form highly productive Power of Two alliances are those with strong internal partnering cultures already in place. These cultures have developed intranetworks, which revolve around a wide variety of internal alliances between or with the following:

- Colleagues (friends who are professional peers)
- Teams linked together to share information, resources, people, and the like
- Resource providers (ranging from department heads to corporate librarians; anyone who can provide needed information)
- Mentors, who can support and facilitate career growth within the organization
- Departments (groups that have learned to work cross-functionally and transcend their functional differences)

Intranetworked organizations are brilliant at partnering with customers, community groups, and competitors; they've learned to think in win-win rather than win-lose terms. People in these companies are constantly exploring new partnerships and effectively managing current ones. There are no off-limit potential allies. Planning sessions are routinely held in which ideas for expanding the infrastructure network are discussed.

Over time, these cultures inculcate values that make Power of Two principles second nature. People in these organizations don't fret over who's getting the best deal or what they don't want to tell their partners. They understand the importance of trust and equality, and this understanding fosters mutually beneficial alliances.

Sometimes the cultural shift is enormous. Traditional companies typically have cultures that focus on being number one, winning at any cost, and dominating the competition. The shift in intranet-worked cultures is toward helping the network win, toward forming alliances with equally powerful individuals and organizations rather than seeking power for power's sake. Sometimes the goal shifts from being number one in a market to being the best partner possible.

The other advantage of all this—besides facilitating the formation and management of external Power of Two alliances—is that it helps companies move toward a flatter, team-based model. Developing a partnering culture is one way to make the transition to values and structures of twenty-first century organizations. As partnering becomes a way of corporate life, the old hierarchies and functional silos begin to crumble.

A Necessary Diversity of Relationships

Psychological and practical barriers prevent organizations from exploring alliances not only with competitors but with companies that are either much smaller or larger than they are, that have different cultures, values, or philosophies, or that are located in another country.

Here are some common objections to partnering with companies different from one's own:

- The small company has very little to offer—fewer dollars, expertise, contacts.

- Little organizations have incompatible cultures—they're mavericks who decide things by the seat of their pants rather than relying on strategy and tactics.

- Big companies will never treat small companies as equals.

- A big corporation is less able to move quickly and flexibly.

- It's impossible to form strong one-on-one relationships with all sorts of companies located in all sorts of countries.

- The cultural clashes with global network partners would be frequent and frustrating.

- The difficulty of coordinating many global allies is daunting.

- One ally has a top-down management style but another is structurally flatter than a pancake.

- A would-be partner is too politically correct—or not politically correct enough.

- One partner makes decisions after lots of debate and discussion; the other is full of one-minute managers.

If you're interested in forming Power of Two alliances, however, you need to move beyond these fears, prejudices, and excuses. If you only ally yourself with an organization just like your own (or that you can dominate or serve), you put yourself at an enormous disadvantage. If you ignore the possibility of a global network, you miss opportunities to leverage contacts in markets with which you're unfamiliar. The odds are that a culturally dissimilar company out there possesses a crucial bit of knowledge that can help you break open a new market, and that a smaller or larger company somewhere owns a brilliant concept you've been searching for in vain. Relationship diversity is perhaps the most timely advantage of the five listed in this chapter. The specific resource, idea, technology, or information one company needs can be discovered by looking in unlikely places. It's impossible to know these days which relationships will yield riches, which is why all types of relationships need to be explored. This can be seen clearly if you understand the changing nature of alliances between big and small companies.

In the past, small companies always wanted to get "in" with big companies. A relationship with a Fortune 500 powerhouse meant access to new markets, vast resources, distribution muscle, and a variety of other advantages. The clout of a big corporation almost made it worth being a subservient partner. Small companies put up with a lot—being excluded from decisions that affected them, carrying out the big partner's dictates, not being listened to, and so on.

Though teaming with large organizations still offers advantages, it also burdens small companies with unwanted baggage. Big organizations often are unable to react swiftly and innovatively in today's changing marketplace; decisions get bogged down in red tape and new products and services aren't created as quickly as they need to be. At the same time, small firms now offer large corporations a variety of advantages. Many of the best and brightest corporate minds have fled their organizations, either downsized or disgusted with moribund cultures. They've formed energetic and creative consultancies and companies that have pioneered technological solutions, service breakthroughs, and entrepreneurial strategies. All this means that the atmosphere is perfect for alliances between big and small. Each has something the other needs and, more so now than ever, it's a fair exchange.

Perhaps the biggest stumbling block to a Power of Two alliance between David and Goliath is miscommunication. Here's an example:

A small company that delivers technology services wanted to align with a much larger organization to help develop new business opportunities in a market it was targeting. The large organization would also benefit, in that its customers were searching for the state-of-the-art technology services offered by the smaller, innovative company. But when the president of the small company attempted to start talks with people at the larger one, he was met with everything from polite inaction to brusque refusal. It was as if he were talking to people who didn't understand his language. Or rather they didn't understand the Power of Two alliance language he was speaking. When the president talked about exploring mutual opportunities, the executives at the large corporation thought he was just asking for money and other resources.

The breakthrough came when he heard that the large corporation had recently hired an alliance champion—an individual empowered to form alliances with any company if it would result in win-win scenarios. After meeting with the champion and developing a solid relationship, a Power of Two alliance was created based on a value proposition (discussed later in the book).

The point is that companies don't have relationships, people do. Alliances are not formed between a large company and a small one, but between two champions who are the same size.

No matter how diverse two partners might be, the alliance can be managed by champions. In fact, Power of Two alliances can accommodate many diverse organizations within its infrastructure network. We'd like to describe one such network from the perspective of Clarke Poynton Grosser, an executive outplacement and coaching firm. John Poynton, a partner at the firm, had been talking with a competitor about a Power of Two alliance network that would span the globe. His vision was to assemble the best executive search firms in the world into a coalition that would share knowledge about best practices, brainstorm and create shared products and services, and open the door for opportunities in new markets. The two firms recognized they needed an alliance champion to make this concept work. Not having anyone in their own organizations who could fill this role, they went outside and hired a champion.

This champion began interviewing key people at other executive outplacement and career development firms, searching for quality organizations with the right values who might join the budding alliance. Over time one firm after another was added, and they coalesced into an alliance of eighteen companies called Manchester Partners. This alliance has undertaken a number of projects and initiated actions that have been beneficial for each participating company, including the following:

- *Benchmarking.* Each company has compared and contrasted best practices, resulting in continual-improvement programs.
- *Development of knowledge capital.* Allies exchange ideas, news, and innovative concepts that they feel might be of use.
- *Quarterly meetings and training sessions.* These are designed to encourage a regular back-and-forth flow of expertise.

The result: each member of the alliance has global reach combined with strong local accountability. Allies have helped each other become knowledgeable about and productive in a number of new markets. Manchester's eighteen partners have 127 offices throughout the world, and in the first two years of the alliance's existence it opened up sales and learning opportunities for each member.

Manchester isn't necessarily the Power of Two network paradigm; it's more formally organized and managed than others we've worked with. Many alliances lack official names and don't hire outsiders as champions and managers. What the Manchester alliance does have in common with other networks is the Power of Two model. All the allies subscribe to the use of champions, free exchange of knowledge capital, and flexible network infrastructure, and all are willing to trust the others and treat them as equals.

The New Competitive Advantage

Size conquered all. The first to market won the race. Breakthrough technology ensured years of success. You could compete successfully on price, product benefits, and image. These truisms have proved to be less true in recent years. We're competing in an age of increasing parity. It's difficult to partner with someone and hope your combined size, technological savvy, or product benefits will win the day.

The five advantages presented in this chapter probably can be acquired in a variety of ways. We've found, however, that Power of Two alliances are one of the fastest, most effective ways. Just about any organization can form and manage a Power of Two alliance, and the following chapters present a process for doing so.

Chapter Three

An Overview of the
Alliance Process

The Power of Two process we present here is designed to be flexible. Because each organization is different, you must shape the process to fit the character and strategy of your organization. This is by no means the only process; if you've done much work with alliances in the past you're probably familiar with at least one other. As you'll see, however, this one is different in many respects. We also hope you'll come to share our belief that it's better.

First, however, you need to understand what the process involves—its chronology, tools, techniques, and illustrative stories. We'd also like to talk about some of the best practices we have developed and observed in alliances over the years. Let's start by listing the elements of the Power of Two process:

- Build the alliance infrastructure within your organization.
- Develop your alliance strategy.
- Create new business opportunities.
- Capitalize on the opportunities by delivering solutions to customers, creating a new technology, making inroads in a new market, or in other ways.
- Manage the alliance relationship.

Now let's look at these elements in greater depth. As we do so, we'll complete a chart showing how they build and feed back on each other.

Building the Alliance Infrastructure

Figure 3.1

Who is going to work on alliances within your organization? This is the first question you should ask, and the one that many companies answer incorrectly. We recommend that the people you choose to develop the alliance strategy and to manage alliances be part of, or closely aligned with, the business unit they will support. The alliance champion also needs to be in or associated with the business unit. That way the business unit has its skin in the game.

If you have a large corporation or organization with multiple business units that will be implementing an alliance strategy, you may want to create a central organization that can leverage some of the infrastructure requirements of an alliance and enable each business unit to capitalize on the best practices of the others. The people in this centralized alliance group don't have to be in the same business unit; they don't have to work for the same manager or dedicate all their time to alliance strategies. They must, however, be ready to provide service to the business unit as needed. A key to Power of Two alliances is speed, and a cumbersome alliance bureaucracy can slow things down.

Even the biggest corporations with the most ambitious alliance strategies shouldn't burden themselves with an alliance management hierarchy. What you want is a small team with diverse expertise. Most companies—especially smaller ones—don't require full-time alliance experts. For instance, unless you're a big corporation you probably don't need a full-time attorney or contracts administrator in your alliance group. In fact, when companies create large dedicated groups of people to support their alliance strategy it's usually because of the lack of attention they receive from a legal, purchasing, or contracts group. Building dedicated groups to support your alliance strategy, however, will not only slow you down but drive up the cost of implementing it. This in turn raises management's expectations of immediate returns from the alliances to justify the expense. So you want to keep support costs to a minimum, especially when you are in start-up mode.

When you're starting to build a Power of Two alliance core group, think of people who are great relationship builders, not great paper pushers:

> We worked on an alliance project with a business unit that was part of a large corporation, and it was new to alliances. It hired new people from other organizations with considerable partnering experience who decided they needed their own contracts, policies, and procedures. As the unit was in start-up mode, we advised drawing upon the alliance resources of the parent company for these things. But our clients insisted that their business model was different. They wanted control over the resources. As a result the alliance people in the business unit were overwhelmed with designing teaming and nondisclosure agreements. When they found a prospective alliance partner they spent inordinate amounts of time negotiating the minutia that come with any collaborative agreement. They established the criterion that they wouldn't team with a company unless it accepted and signed their alliance agreement. Things that needed attention, such as the development of relationships with other champions and of new business opportunities, suffered.

> It should come as no surprise that this business unit drove some of its prospective alliance partners to the competition. After all, the prospective partners reasoned, if this company is difficult to work with now, imagine how awful it will be if we forge an alliance. Many of the alliance partners had good working relationships with the parent organization and were surprised and disappointed that the parent did not step in to give some stern guidance.

The issue here was leverage. The business unit had the opportunity to leverage the alliance infrastructure of the parent company. The value in alliance relationships is in the relationships, not the contracts.

Another organizational requisite is choosing an alliance champion. This person could be part of a business unit, a member of corporate staff, or a third party. Whoever you select should have strong ties to the business unit. Otherwise the champion will be like any other staff person who is on the outside trying to tell the unit how to conduct its business inside.

A champion should be thoroughly familiar with the value proposition of the business unit, the gaps in customer offerings, and the culture of your organization. True champions possess highly developed interpersonal skills, and they're masters at building strong relationships with their counterparts at other organizations. In Chapter Five, we discuss the role and characteristics of the alliance champion in detail and suggest ways to identify who might fill the role effectively.

The organization we just discussed, which created its own contracts and agreements instead of leveraging its parent company's infrastructure, decided to put its champion for a particular group of potential alliance partners into a "business partner organization":

> Potential alliance partners started to bring new business opportunities to the champion, a former sales manager who unfortunately still acted like one much of the time. For this discussion we'll call him the alliance sales manager.
>
> When the alliance sales manager approached his company's customer sales organization about teaming with this new set of alliance partners, he met a lot of resistance. He was new to the organization, so the customer sales managers didn't know him or trust him. Although the organization had aligned the goals of the customer sales team with those of the alliance sales team, the two teams had not formulated a joint alliance plan to set expectations for what

value the new alliance partners would bring to customers and to the organization.

Thus the customer sales management team held to its old paradigm regarding control of the customer selling situation. The new alliance partners found it difficult and frustrating to work with the alliance sales manager because he didn't leverage them within his organization. He was constantly selling internally (and asking the alliance partners to help with that) instead of focusing on outside market opportunities.

If this alliance sales manager had been inside the customer sales organization, his company might have gained a stranglehold on the market by demonstrating greater value to the customer base. It could have reacted quicker and become the preferred alliance partner. Instead it opened the door for the competition to work with this set of alliance partners.

The organization still might have failed, for the alliance sales manager did not have the right skills to lead a Power of Two alliance. Again, we will go into detail on these skills in Chapter Five.

As you probably know, lawyers play major roles in traditional partnering arrangements. They can hold them up for weeks or months with various stipulations. Most lawyers don't operate with a Power of Two mentality. They're trained to protect their client, not to create a mutually beneficial agreement.

We'll not spend a lot of time talking about lawyers in alliances, but we would like to say a few words here because they do serve a role, and it doesn't have to be a negative one. In Power of Two alliances, their proper role is to use their legal expertise to protect and preserve the alliance (rather than just the company). They make the alliance easier to form rather than throwing obstacles in the path to its formation:

We worked with a manufacturing company that decided to branch out its alliance relationships to some service companies that could help it bring more complete solutions to its customers. The service companies also worked with the manufacturer's competitors, however—an arrangement new to the manufacturer. It was thus wary of sharing information with the service companies, so its corporate legal group created a number of contracts to protect it. These lawyers had very little practical experience in teaming, and they quickly alienated the service companies.

Fortunately, a lawyer in the manufacturer's field sales organization had extensive alliance experience and stepped in to save the day. Recognizing the sensitivities of the service organizations, he called himself a contracts negotiator rather than an attorney so as to focus both sides on the business issues involved. Only after those were resolved were the legal issues addressed. When a legal issue emerged that could have exposed the manufacturer to risk, rather than jump the gun and confront the service company the lawyer referred it to his corporate legal staff for analysis and recommendations. Only then did he bring the issue to the service company and ask for help in working it out. A less alliance-experienced lawyer might have been less flexible: "Take it out of the contract or we don't have a deal." As he did have a lot of experience working with alliances it was an easy transition for him to put together the teaming agreements with the service companies. And as he was the single point of contact for the first few teaming arrangements, the alliance champion used him as a subject matter expert for agreements in different parts of the country.

At the other end of the spectrum, consider this case:

A product company decided to go from a "we-can-do-it-all" strategy to a "we-need-alliance-partners" strategy to grow its market and deliver the value its customers were demanding. The company rushed to the market, arms open to all kinds of potential alliances. But it had given little thought to the resources required to support this new strategy: relationship management, technical support, and administrative (including legal) support. The lawyer who had supported all contract needs of the direct customer sales organization now supported the needs of the alliance organization as well. He had no experience dealing with alliance partners and, as it turned out, no time to work with them either; they went to the bottom of his priority list. Nor did the new alliance organization have the clout to change his mind; the plan it had submitted to management did not consider the need for additional support resources. When the legal counsel eventually did hire a couple of attorneys to support him, they too had no experience working with alliances. Business opportunities that the alliance partners brought forth were delayed because the lawyers were unable to respond quickly and in an alliance-friendly manner.

Another value that the central administration organization provides is to develop the documentation required to support the alliance initiatives of the alliance champion. This documentation should be general enough that it can be used by all the business units to form specific alliances. Some of the documents required for use outside the organization are subcontracts, teaming agreements, and nondisclosure agreements. The availability of these, even in draft form, helps keep the alliance champions focused on relationship and business development instead of on alliance formalities. What's important here is to have not just documentation but partner-friendly documentation. That means the champion and the legal staff must create documentation (or modify whatever has been used for alliances before) to ensure it creates a win-win situation for all sides in the alliance. If you don't have alliance documentation, approach one of the alliance partners and propose to adopt its documents instead of creating your own. This is an example of the openness and knowledge sharing necessary in a Power of Two alliance.

Another member of the alliance team should handle contract administration. Again we won't dwell on this, but it's important to touch on because members of Power of Two alliances are very good communicators, and a good contract administrator facilitates information flow throughout the organization. We have seen some contract administrators put in place to protect the assets of the company, create policies and procedures, and otherwise impede the Power of Two alliance process. We advocate someone objective and with an independent voice to advise and counsel champions.

If you have an extensive alliance network—if your company forms a variety of Power of Two alliances over the course of a year—you need to keep track of all your agreements. This ensures for the organization that there is no duplication or conflict of interest between alliance partners. For example, if Business Unit A signs an alliance agreement with a services company, then Business Unit B should be able to take advantage of that agreement if it also chooses to have an alliance with the same services company. But B won't know that A has such an agreement unless someone in the organization is tracking all agreements. A contracts administration manager is a resource the alliance champion can rely on to find out if alliance relationships are in place that can now be leveraged. The champion may learn that other alliance agreements of various types have been put in place by other champions, and may be able to work with champions in other business units and learn from their experience. Another example: if Business Unit A believes it needs to sign an exclusive agreement with a products company, the contracts administration group can either verify that the agreement does not conflict with the alliance strategies of other business units or (more likely) inform Unit A and the alliance champion that signing exclusive alliance agreements is outside the organization's strategy.

Here's a revealing case:

Two companies put together an agreement with a customer on the east coast to build a custom order management and distribution system that included technologies proprietary to each. The customer saw this as a competitive advantage and insisted that the two companies sign an agreement not to sell the new system to anyone else in the customer's industry. The two companies went along; it seemed a great opportunity. The agreement was put together by the local sales organization of each company. Neither involved their alliance champions, though this was the first time the two companies had teamed. About three months later, one of the companies was preparing to sign a contract with another customer in the southwest to use the company's proprietary technology with a different alliance partner. Sorry, said the corporate attorneys; they'd discovered the earlier, exclusive agreement with the first customer. Using the technology with the new customer would violate it. As the first customer stuck to its guns, the company was shut out of a market.

The corporate or central organizations in a company many times are viewed as business inhibitors. But when you get into the alliance business they can provide leverage for the whole organization.

Besides monitoring alliance agreements, a contracts administrator can create and share knowledge capital across the organization. Through regular communications with alliance champions or by creating an electronic bulletin board, they can keep everyone aware of agreements, common terms, and lessons learned. Alliance champions also have the opportunity to use this bulletin board to share their experiences.

Other groups within the organization that will have an impact on alliance strategy and implementation are public relations, purchasing, and corporate marketing. As part of the alliance start-up process the champion should figure out who in each of these areas will be able to provide the support alliances need. Again, the champion needs to be astute about who are good team players that will grasp the importance of work for the alliance rather than the organization. The designated alliance supporters don't need to spend a great deal of time on alliance issues at first; they simply need to be briefed and ready to lend a hand when their services are required.

Developing Your Alliance Strategy

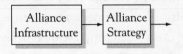

Figure 3.2

Your organization may already have relationships or alliance partners. You may have had some success and perhaps many failures. At times you may even have doubted the partnering strategy. We hear this often. You have not achieved your goals for market growth, profitability, or global expansion, but you have teamed with your business partners many times. One advantage, though, is that you've already made some mistakes and know that your current strategy is not working. This is the opportunity to rethink that strategy and take action. If you are new to alliances, then you won't have to fix anything. You can start from scratch.

To make the transition to a business strategy that incorporates a relationship-based alliance strategy requires the support of the executive team. Here's an example:

> The executive team at a Fortune 1000 company recently realized that it needed to change its business model from transactions, discounts, and end-of-quarter deals to one based on relationships. Revenue was declining; customers needed to see more than an economic value to the company's product. Management recognized that it needed to start partnering with companies that help add value to the customer. Members of the executive team were so committed to this new strategy that they visited key customers, as well as executives of their current partners, to deliver their alliance message. To back up this change, they revamped the compensation criteria for everyone in the organization. They sent the message that every employee is a relationship manager, from the CEO down to the local sales representative, and that compensation would be based on that new role.

It will take some time for this company to establish the trust and confidence of its alliance partners both at the executive level and the local level. The important thing is that it changed its strategy and the executives made personal commitments to their customers and their alliance partners.

After securing the executive team's involvement, the next step is to create a leveraged network, harnessing the power of your internal and external network. Alliance champions evaluate their internal networks by looking for the following people (including the aforementioned involved executives):

- *Like-minded supporters*—managers likely to contribute ideas and resources to the alliance effort
- *Knowledge resources*—corporate librarians or other internal knowledge experts
- *Mentors*—individuals of influence within the organization that the alliance can rely on to use their clout and experience
- *Key customers*—customers who have made (or who the champion feels could make) the transition to a relationship-based alliance
- *Key suppliers*—suppliers who have made or could make the transition to a relationship-based alliance
- *Supportive administrative staff*—people within the organization who will help grease the alliance wheels and make it a bit easier for the alliance to move forward quickly and flexibly

Champions also need to examine who in their external network they can rely on for assistance, including these:

- *Industry influencers*—leaders in your industry and complementary industries who have access and influence with a diverse number of organizations and individuals
- *Suppliers and customers of industry influencers*—often overlooked as outsiders or unreachables; champions know they're

only one contact away and use their relationship-building skills to gain their trust and cooperation

- *External knowledge experts*—including people such as professors, consultants, authors, columnists, trade association executives; anyone who can supply critical data and ideas that grant insight about what partners and opportunities to pursue

The Power of Two process also requires a thorough and perceptive alliance analysis, with the goal of identifying what you're missing, what a partner might add, and how the synergistic mix might better help you achieve your business objectives. For many organizations this analysis centers on a company's value proposition in relation to customers—the unique combinations of skills, capabilities, and products and services you currently offer your existing and potential customers. To make your alliance strategy truly customer-driven, you need to identify the gaps in your offerings and potential ways to fill them by partnering with another company. As you might expect, Power of Two companies analyze alliance possibilities with a different set of criteria than traditional alliances. Instead of only looking at what the alliance will give them, they evaluate what the alliance will mean to customers, suppliers, and their alliance partner; they assess whether an alliance will supply them with missing knowledge, ideas, technologies, and other avenues into opportunity. Instead of analyzing alliances solely in terms of short-term profits, the analysis methodology will give you a much more holistic way to consider your options.

Once the analysis is complete and you've established the criteria to choose a partner, the process kicks into high gear. A series of issues arise that must be examined so that once you've chosen the right partner you can maintain a productive relationship. The success (or failure) of the alliance depends on addressing the following:

Creating Rules of Engagement. Power of Two alliances don't operate by the seat of their champions' pants. Important policies and procedures are discussed and determined in advance. A certain amount of structure helps allies move quickly and confidently when opportunities arise (rather than wasting time debating the whos, whats, wheres, and whys). We'll provide you with some effective Power of Two rules and techniques for establishing them in Chapter Eight.

Trust. A Power of Two alliance without trust isn't a Power of Two alliance. You can have everything else in place, but if either party suspects the other's motives, feels that the other is getting more than its fair share, or feels misled or deceived, then the alliance won't be effective. How to build a strong bond of trust will be discussed in detail in Chapter Nine.

Culture and Communication. No two cultures are alike. There are both subtle and obvious differences, and when companies start working together these different styles of working and communicating can loom large. Part of the Power of Two process is for companies to recognize and acknowledge these differences. It's not that Power of Two companies have similar cultures; it's that they learn to work with each other's particular way of doing things and establish an alliance culture that works for both.

Creating New Business Opportunities

Figure 3.3

Power of Two alliances cocreate opportunities in a wide variety of ways, and we'll discuss how you can apply this cocreating methodology to your collaborative efforts more thoroughly in Chapter Seven. One thing we'll focus on is making that first opportunity count. It sets the tone for the alliance. You don't have to win the business, break open a new market, or come up with a brilliant breakthrough concept when you first cocreate. The important thing is for you and your alliance partner to demonstrate commitment to each other's success as you focus on the opportunity.

Champions, of course, play a key role in building that commitment. They need to be intimately involved with the details of the first few business opportunities; they need to be out there in the trenches doing everything possible to help the alliance achieve its objective. If something goes wrong between the respective field organizations, neophyte allies have very few deposits in the emotional bank account to fall back on. There will be little trust until there is success. Champions need to keep everyone focused on the opportunity and avoid distractions caused by relationship issues and process glitches.

The success factors, the role of the alliance champion, rules of engagement, communications, culture, and building trust each play a prominent role in the development of new opportunities with your alliance partners.

Capitalize on the Opportunities

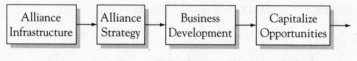

Figure 3.4

The whole purpose of your alliance strategy is to deliver something to your customers, your organization, or the marketplace. In our chapter on cocreating opportunities, we'll talk about how alliances have delivered meaningful results based on the opportunities they've cocreated. We stress "meaningful" because some partnerships simply deliver results; they accomplish minor goals rather than major ones or they make money once from a project but never again. Short-term, dead-end results are not what Power of Two alliances are about.

As we discuss throughout the following chapters, alliances need to be clear about what they want the opportunity to achieve. In

Chapter Eight on rules of engagement, for instance, we'll explain why it's crucial that champions set ambitious, mutually desirable objectives and that they go after appropriate opportunities.

Manage the Alliance Relationship

Figure 3.5

Too many alliance strategies concentrate on finding partners to the exclusion of managing the relationship. It's almost as if the strategic thinkers feel that the alliance will manage itself. Take our word for it: it won't.

This last element in the process is one we stress because Power of Two alliances need to function well even when opportunities aren't being pursued. A good deal of activity in Power of Two alliances consists of knowledge sharing—the back-and-forth communication of ideas and information. It's from this knowledge sharing that opportunities often spring, and champions recognize that it's essential to keep that knowledge flowing smoothly. They understand that if relationships sour or conflict flares they can't ignore it or deal with it superficially. Champions are wizards at managing the alliance relationship, and in our discussion of champions (Chapter Five) we'll provide a number of ideas that will help you manage issues that can prove fatal to alliances.

Managing the relationship also means defining success criteria. Will success be based on new business, increased market share? In what industries, in what geographies? Or will it be based on knowledge sharing, and if so, how will you measure success for both parties? Setting the expectations, talking about them frequently, and reexamining success criteria are all part of what Power of Two allies routinely do. The performance of the alliance will be determined by the goals you set up front for all parties involved. When you conduct alliance assessments is a good time to define and document success for your company and your alliance partners. How you will monitor alliance performance and how often (monthly, quarterly, or yearly) it will be reviewed are necessary decisions to be made for the long-term health of the relationship.

Managing the relationship means asking tough questions and discussing the answers with your partner. Some of these questions include the following:

- Do our alliance problems get resolved quickly?
- Is it easy for us to work together?
- Does the alliance champion follow up?
- Are our points of contact well defined?
- Is our alliance partner biased toward our competitors?
- Do we know where we are going with the alliance in the future?
- Has our direction changed since the alliance's inception and is the change acceptable?
- Are we following the rules of engagement we set forth?
- Should the alliance be renegotiated? Canceled? Do we need to change alliance champions?

Define Best Practices

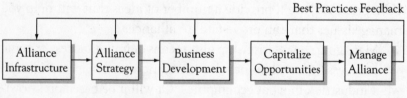

Figure 3.6

As you become familiar with this process and implement it in your own Power of Two strategy, don't expect to do everything perfectly the first time. When we help companies partner we always tell them that they need to capture best practices as well as worst practices. Each process element represents an area where you'll want to develop best practices, and if you chart what takes place as you move through the process you'll be able to do so.

Designate someone to capture best practices as they occur. The quarterly or annual meeting that you schedule with your alliance partner to review the status of each alliance is a good time to do a best practices review. During this meeting, champions should make specific points as opposed to giving general observations in describing how things are going. Use concrete examples to illustrate points.

Invariably this review yields eye-opening information. Companies learn that they tend not to take certain rules of engagement seriously. They discover that they haven't done a good job of building trust. They find that they're extremely irritated by certain cultural issues (the way the other company communicates, for instance) and haven't done a good job addressing these issues in advance. They may also find that they've done a terrific job in their selection criteria for champions and in the way they cocreate opportunities. Building the best practices back into the alliance infrastructure and changing or eliminating the worst practices should become a reflex action.

As you read, keep a mental or written checklist of your current best and worst practices as they relate to the process issues being discussed. Make it a habit to think about what you're doing that facilitates Power of Two strategies as well as how you might inadvertently be thwarting these strategies. Power of Two allies share their best practices knowledge, and this always results in a stronger alliance both for the partners and for other companies they collaborate with in the future.

Chapter Four

Leveraged Networks

Most people are members of internal and external networks. Within their organizations, they've formed strong relationships with a variety of people who represent numerous functions. Externally, they've established solid relationships with vendors, marketing services agencies, consultants, and the like. Even if these relationships aren't structured as formal alliances—even if we don't have alliance champions to manage these relationships—they provide a network to communicate ideas and information.

Networks are the building blocks of alliances. Someone in Company A has networked with someone in Company B for years; they decide to do a deal together and thus an alliance is born. This alliance, however, may not be the right one for either company. It's been born out of familiarity and the desire to do a deal. There may be many other, better partners out there for each organization.

Power of Two alliances don't just evolve out of networks; they grow out of leveraged networks. A leveraged network is rich with knowledge and resources that you lack. It's a network filled with people you want to work with who lead you to other people you want to work with. It's a network that gives you access to opportunities you would otherwise miss out on. And, of course, it's a network that runs both ways—you offer others resources and opportunities that they lack. When it's time to form a Power of Two alliance, your network is the place where you'll find a worthy ally.

Creating a leveraged network is not a random, haphazard process. For leveraging to work, it has to be done strategically and with certain goals in mind. There are many possible ways to find worthwhile contacts to become part of your network; for some examples, see Table 4.1.

Let's look at how to create a leveraged network strategy.

A Six-Step Process

Begin by thinking in one-on-one terms. When you build a leveraged network, you build it one relationship at a time. That means the goal isn't quantity; it's not just working your network and filling up a Rolodex with new names; it's not finding people with prestigious titles from well-known companies whose business cards you can hang on your office wall like scalps.

The goal is twofold: to find people you know who can bridge the gap between what your organization already has and what it needs or may need in the future, and to find people who possess the personalities and mind-sets that dovetail with who you are and how you think. To accomplish these goals, consider the following six steps.

1. *Analyze your organization for what's missing.* What are your company's strengths? Its weaknesses? Analyze your core competencies. What competencies do your competitors possess that you lack? What competencies does everyone lack that may be important in the future? What type of knowledge do you wish you had—what facts, figures, research, and the like would it be useful to know about? Does your company suffer from a lack of creativity, of fresh ideas and thinking? What resources—technological, economic, cognitive, geographic— would it be valuable to possess?

2. *Analyze your current network to determine if it can supply what's missing.* Start out by creating a list of names of all the people you interact with regularly, both internally and externally. Focus on who might be able to supply what you're missing. In considering this, remember that a person can fill in your

Table 4.1. Networking Levels Matrix.

MegaNetworking Networking Levels Matrix			
Baseline	**Qualifications**	**Prospecting**	**Collaborations**
Professional networking groups	Industry association meetings	Regular follow-up with referral sources	Creating new business ventures with associates
Political and community fundraisers and events	Events with targeted influencers in attendance	Scheduled meetings with associates	Cross-selling with associates
Civic organization meetings	Target market's organizations of influence meetings	Employ growth stages of a relationship	Strategic alliances
Friends and relatives	Meetings with qualified prospects	Leverage your relationships	

Source: Service Showcase, Inc., 2300 N. Barrington Rd., Ste. 400, Hoffman Estates, Illinois, 60195.

company's blanks indirectly as well as directly. By indirectly, we mean that they may lead you to another person who can meet your needs. In addition, don't focus only on obvious, tangible things such as money and technology. Useful information can be worth more than a pile of gold, so identify who has information you lack. Think about which people might supply you with knowledge capital—with ideas and information that would be difficult to obtain elsewhere.

3. *Analyze your current network based on individual attitudes and behaviors.* We can't stress enough that Power of Two alliances are one-on-one relationships. Similarly, a leveraged network involves relationships between individuals, not companies. Determine which individuals are proactive, open to new ideas, and regularly offering you new information and the chance to meet new people.

4. *Form a primary network.* This step moves your networking efforts toward a successful alliance, as the networking matrix in Table 4.1 shows. The goal is to choose no more than ten people from your list. These people give you the best chance of obtaining needed resources now and in the future. They are individuals you're excited about working with. Even if you're not quite sure how they can help your organization, you respond positively to their energy and ideas and look forward to partnering with them at some point. Winnowing your network down to a manageable number is critical. It focuses your time and attention on the relationships that can do you the most good.

5. *Communicate regularly with your network.* Meet or talk on the phone at least once a month. Exchange ideas and information. This communication establishes a level of trust that is crucial for future alliances. It also gets both parties thinking about possible opportunities. Just as importantly, these exchanges are good tests of how well (or poorly) you work together.

6. *Explore possible opportunities*. Is there a current business opportunity you might pursue together? Is there an opportunity you might cocreate? Can a member of your network introduce you to someone who might help you with an opportunity? Though you haven't formed an alliance, you can think and talk in terms of opportunities. Just thinking and talking this way can build your relationship and give you a sense of whether an alliance is feasible.

After going through these six steps you'll have established a leveraged network. It will open doors that were closed. You'll find yourself meeting people who seemed inaccessible and learning about new markets, technologies, and strategies. The other people in the network will challenge you in ways you've never been challenged before. Ideally, if an alliance forms, these people will be the champions.

Implementing the Process

Here is an excellent example of implementation:

> Danilo Inc., a small import-export company, was concerned by increased competition from multinational companies. This was its impetus to build a leveraged network. Danilo assessed the hundreds of companies it did business with and that could be considered part of a loosely structured network. After doing his homework, Danilo's champion found four other companies that seemed ideally suited to be part of a leveraged network. Interestingly, all four were competitors of roughly the same size as Danilo. Their strengths, however, nicely balanced Danilo's and each other's weaknesses. One of the companies was skilled at training employees on new federal regulations; another was accomplished at sponsoring legislation at the local and state levels; a third had a presence in a number of key ports.
>
> There was also a nice fit between the representatives of each company. Danilo's champion had eliminated a number of companies

from consideration because their representatives had seemed secretive and inflexible and exhibited other traits that didn't fit with the leveraged network concept. Danilo's champion and the other three representatives, though all had different personalities and perspectives, shared a willingness to exchange ideas and information. That's exactly what they did after establishing their primary network. Then, almost a year after forming their network, Danilo's champion and another member of the network began investigating an opportunity that arose in China. The opportunity intrigued them because together they had the right combination of resources to take advantage of it—a combination even their larger multinational competitors lacked. After exploring the opportunity from a number of angles, the two companies formed a Power of Two alliance and have not only profited from it but gained insights and experience that will enable them to repeat this success in the future.

Unleveraged Networks

We don't want to make the six-step process sound easier than it is. All sorts of networking and relationship-building approaches exist, and some of them yield very different types of alliances than the one we're proposing. Traps and obstacles loom along the leveraged network path, and we'd like to tell you about the most dangerous ones:

Confusing Activity with Accomplishment. Leveraged networks are not passive; they are designed to lead the members of the network toward productive alliances. Networking, however, often translates as "working the room" and amassing collections of business cards. All this activity is worthless unless it is done systematically and with a sense of purpose.

Prioritizing Quantity over Quality. When people operate under the misconception that the bigger the network the better the results, they end up with an unwieldy primary network. Ten or fewer partners is the rule for a leveraged network. If chosen well, these partners will help you find all the opportunities you can handle.

Lack of a Plan. "Networking is simple; you just go out and do it" is the philosophy here. The problem, of course, is that you leave who you network with to chance. It's like running a business without a strategy. The six-step process is designed to yield a network in which every member can leverage each other's strengths, ideas, and people.

Unequal Participation. Some organizations form good networks but then sit back and wait for other members of the network to bring them ideas and opportunities. Leveraged networks demand mutual exchanges of ideas and information. When one member is always the receiver of ideas and another generates them, it's bound to fall apart before an alliance can be formed.

Short-Term Focus. Networks that form with a deal-making mentality never become leveraged networks. Either they dissolve quickly when there's no immediate payback or later when the payback they achieved at the start isn't repeated. Leveraged networks are visionary; they are willing to explore and investigate ideas, developing mutual goals that may not be achieved for months or years. Leveraging is much easier when every partner has had the time to learn to trust everyone else in the network. This makes everyone more willing to make commitments and share resources.

The Human Factor

The concept of leveraged networks often drives people to look for synergistic resources. In other words, they attempt to establish relationships with organizations that result in a high-energy mix of strengths. They're excited when they find and begin exchanging ideas with companies that seem to be perfect partners. The only problem is that though the companies may be perfect partners, the individuals representing them may not. The word "network" suggests a connection, and that connection must be between people, not just resources. Consider this case:

We know of two high-tech companies that were ideally suited to work together: an Internet site design firm and a software company that created applications for the Internet. There were all sorts of possibilities for collaboration, and it seemed inevitable that they would form an alliance at some point. Three other companies in a loosely structured network had brought these two potential members together, certain they would not only add to the network but collaborate well together. The relationship managers for both companies, however, were incompatible. One was a nuts-and-bolts guy who favored direct talk and simple solutions. The other was a pontificator who bogged down in the complexity of his thinking. From the start, they couldn't stand each other. Still, they attempted to force the relationship, recognizing the potential synergy between their two organizations and hoping that being members of a larger network would lessen the tension between them. It didn't work. Both relationship managers went out of their way to avoid meeting with or talking to each other; they handled most communication through e-mail and faxes. Eventually they stopped communicating altogether.

The point is to remember the Power of Two concept. Even in networks, one-on-one relationships are the glue that holds everything together. Without a strong bond of trust and communication between two key people an alliance will never get off the ground. Leveraged networks are possible only when the people in those networks work well together. That doesn't mean the people are all alike. In fact, most leveraged networks benefit from the differences between members—the different perspectives and personalities rubbing together produce creative sparks.

But if you can't stand another person in your network, it's tough to leverage the people, knowledge, and other resources he represents. The following will help avoid networking with the wrong people:

- *View personality extremes as a yellow flag.* Leveraged networks can consist of up to ten members, and it only takes one extreme personality to disrupt the network. Admittedly, "extreme" is a subjective term, and you don't want to eliminate anyone just for having an excess of a given trait. Still, we've found that highly dominant and highly cautious people can do serious damage to a network. In the former case, people can't stand their bossiness. In the latter, they can't tolerate their indecisiveness.

- *Foster a high degree of personality awareness, both of yourself and others.* What's your personality style? What is the style of someone you might network with? Personality tests such as the Myers-Briggs Type Indicator can formally answer these questions and help you assess compatibility. Informally, you should try to interact with people on a number of occasions before including them in your network. Determine if you enjoy dealing with them or if they drive you crazy. Assess whether you're looking forward to doing business with them or dreading it.

- *Establish a method or system for dealing with personality conflicts.* Many conflict management tools exist that might be helpful in this regard. You may also want to establish ground rules in advance to deal with misunderstandings, irritating habits, and other problems. Leveraged networks function best when major points of tension between members are dealt with quickly and effectively.

Giving and Receiving Knowledge

At the heart of every leveraged network is a knowledge exchange. This isn't just an admirable concept, and it's not something done every so often or randomly. Without the continual and clear exchange of knowledge capital there's little to leverage. Alliances are formed and opportunities are seized when network members receive a nugget of knowledge that opens their eyes. In most instances, it's knowledge they would never have obtained on their own. A new bit of information causes the receiver to think, "What if . . . ?" That what-if is explored and analyzed and may lead to talks with another network member about a collaboration.

Here are some suggestions for facilitating the exchange of knowledge in a network:

- *Schedule informal as well as formal meetings.* Official meetings are fine, but more relaxed interactions can often be beneficial. Internet and Intranet communication and social gatherings at restaurants and bars are just a few of the alternatives available to network members. The "Friends and Family" ad campaign from MCI, for instance, grew out of conversations that took place at a bar across the street from MCI headquarters. At Andersen Consulting, social spaces are reserved within the office for informal exchanges of ideas and information. From chat rooms to phone calls to teleconferencing, many forums exist for networking partners to talk and brainstorm.

- *Use various tools to catalyze knowledge exchanges.* Sometimes people need a jump-start before they really open up with another person in the network. For instance, we've found a methodology called "Questioneering" to be very effective in stimulating discussions. It involves a facilitator asking people highly unusual and provocative questions (for example, "What would your company be like if your mother were running it?") that get people thinking and talking. Just having a facilitator on-line or in the same room with network partners can enhance the knowledge exchange process.

- *Avoid censorship.* This is the easiest to implement and the hardest to do. The paradox stems from the reality of most corporate cultures, in which certain pieces of information are considered off-limits to outsiders, especially if those outsiders happen to be competitors. In a Power of Two alliance, it's critical that this information be shared and that the sharing be part of the alliance ground rules. A networking situation, however, is a looser collaborative structure. Because you haven't reached the alliance stage, you may be wary about sharing financial or strategic data. Still, if you're completely closed off from others in the network they will respond in kind. As much as possible, you should encourage an exchange of ideas and information.

A Networking Mentality

Networking isn't a skill set that most organizations address in their training or encourage in their culture. Yet it is becoming increasingly important in an interdependent world. In *The Age of the Network* (Oliver White Publications, 1994), Jeffrey Stamps and Jessica Linnack make a case for the network being an appropriate organizational design in the information age, citing its interconnectedness and ability to facilitate an exchange of ideas.

The leveraged network model we're suggesting encourages companies to start making networking a part of their culture and their training. It's a skill that needs to be practiced both internally and externally. A leading sales promotion agency such as Frankel & Company, for instance, has determined that networking is a key leadership skill that it needs to address and that is often absent in younger managers.

Networking shouldn't only be the responsibility of an organization's alliance champion. Others should take the initiative to form knowledge-based relationships. Consider this case:

The sales director of one hospital supply manufacturer is a brilliant networker. He's active in a sales and marketing association, communicates with a variety of entrepreneurs, health industry executives, and other sales people on the Web, and is proactive in seeking out experts in different fields. It's important to note that this sales director isn't a social butterfly; he's making contacts and forming relationships based on two factors: whether he is excited about the possibility of working with a given individual in the future and whether the person has resources, knowledge, or contacts that may prove valuable to his organization. Through his extensive networking, this sales director established his own private network with eight or nine people. Through these people, he learned that there would soon be a great opportunity for a new line of blood testing products. Working with one of these individuals, he helped his company enter into an alliance with his networking counterpart's company to develop the line of products.

None of this would have been possible if the sales director's management hadn't supported his efforts. Organizations need to encourage their people—especially their alliance champions—to develop networking skills and use them. That's tough to do for some bottom-line, hierarchical companies. They're so focused on short-term results and productivity that they don't see the value of networking. They view it as a social activity that yields nothing tangible. It's true that knowledge is intangible, but it translates into very tangible and very profitable results down the line.

To promote a networking mentality, management can do the following:

- Offer networking workshops and other training in this area.
- Encourage networking through various rewards and recognition.
- Make people aware of networking opportunities—social gatherings, Internet possibilities, industry associations and related meetings, and others—through newsletters and other forms of employee communication.

Communicating with Your Network

Once you've established your network, it's important to set some guidelines and exchange some information in order to maximize your leverage. You may have assembled exactly the right people representing exactly the right organizations. But if you don't establish some common ground it will be difficult to take full advantage of what your network has to offer.

The following questions should be asked not only *by* you but *of* you. They will produce information that will enable you and your partners to communicate better and more efficiently.

1. What are your company's top three challenges and opportunities?
2. What is the decision-making process for external relationships (such as alliances) in your company?
3. What are the major trends you see influencing your industry and your organization?
4. How does your company measure success?
5. If you refer me to another company, what would you like to see happen?
6. How can we best stay in contact with one another? What is your favorite method for staying in touch (e-mail, phone, fax, meetings, or others)?
7. When is it inconvenient or difficult for you to network?
8. Which of the top influencers in your industry do you know personally?
9. What is your organization's vision of where it wants to be in three to five years?
10. What is most important to you when you form an alliance or collaborate with another organization?

Chapter Five

The Alliance Champion

Power of Two alliances simply don't work without champions. You may have a perfect fit between partners, tremendous resources, and great opportunities, but you'll never achieve Power of Two status if you don't have champions in place. They're the ones who have the vision and skills to move the alliance forward faster and more flexibly than anyone thought possible. Because they've earned the trust and respect of both organizations, they enjoy the freedom to take risks and suggest bold directions denied to others.

Champions are exceptional people, and the goal of this chapter is to help you understand what makes a champion and what traits to look for so that you make the right choice for your organization. Before examining these traits, however, it's crucial to make the distinction between an alliance champion and a relationship manager.

A Sometimes Subtle, Always Significant Difference

Relationship managers have a role in Power of Two alliances, but they should not be mistaken for champions or substitute for them. Many companies have created relationship manager positions to handle the growing number of collaborative efforts with other organizations, and these people are often drawn from sales or marketing. They usually are skilled at working with other people, negotiate well, present themselves well—and focus on short-term issues. In other words, they are able to manage the nuts and bolts of relationships.

What they lack are some if not all of the big-picture traits of champions. They rarely look five years down the road and envision where an alliance is headed. They don't exhibit the same commitment to goals and willingness to fight to achieve them as champions. They are more likely to make decisions by the seat of their pants instead of relying on a well-conceived plan.

At some point relationship managers may grow into champions. Until they do, however, their responsibilities in Power of Two alliances must be limited to such things as making presentations, establishing contacts at other organizations, conveying and receiving information, serving as an intermediary between the alliance and customers, and keeping track of the alliance budget and various dates and deadlines.

Certainly there's some overlap between the responsibilities of relationship managers and those of champions. It's important, however, to recognize what defines and differentiates a champion. To help you do so, we've created a list of seven skills and characteristics of the type of people who make good alliance champions. Following the list we examine each characteristic or skill in some depth; the examples and tips we provide will help you determine if a given person is qualified to be a champion.

1. Integrity
2. Strategist
3. Visionary
4. Planner
5. Communicator
6. Collaborator
7. Persistence

Integrity

Trust and respect for a champion can hold a Power of Two alliance together when other forces threaten to break it apart. Sometimes alliances have to take certain matters on faith. The decision to pursue an opportunity that has not yet emerged—to invest time, people, and money in a venture with no immediate payoff—requires an unshakable belief. This belief isn't always just in the venture itself, but in the person leading it.

We've seen more than one alliance crumble because the initial trust between partners dissolved. Consider this case, for example:

A relationship manager at a major software company had established an alliance with a service firm. He did a great job finding this partner and working with the service firm to establish the alliance's goals. During the first few months of the relationship both companies freely exchanged information and learned a lot about each other and potentially profitable new markets. As often happens, however, the software company began putting pressure on the relationship manager to produce short-term results. In response, he began exaggerating the number of opportunities the alliance was generating.

In the greater scheme of things, this wasn't that unusual or that dishonest. Hyperbole was a standard tool of the sales people in his company, and he had come up through sales. It's even possible that he believed what he was saying: wishful thinking caused him to turn vague possibilities into real opportunities. Whatever the reason, his reports and presentations revved up management of both the software company and the service firm. It also bought him some time, easing the pressure on him (and on the alliance) to produce short-term results.

Eventually, however, the alliance champion at the service firm discovered that the relationship manager had not only exaggerated the number of opportunities for the alliance but had distorted the truth on a number of other fronts. From this discovery onward, the alliance was never the same. Though it was kept intact for the remainder of the year, the champion (and his company's management) no longer trusted his counterpart. Information was no longer freely exchanged. Decision making slowed. It was difficult to reach consensus on key issues. What had all the potential of being a Power of Two alliance quickly became nothing more than a failed collaboration.

When attempting to determine if candidates for champion possess the necessary integrity, ask the following questions:

- Is there any instance in the past when the candidate violated the values or beliefs of the organization?
- Do you feel the candidate would sacrifice a long-term goal for short-term results?
- Is this person basically honest but willing to stretch or color the truth in order to increase the odds of getting what he wants?
- Do you know of any instance in the candidate's past when she took a strong position based on what she believed (for example, stood up to a superior she felt was acting unethically)?
- Assuming the candidate has done well in his career up to this point, has his straightforwardness, honesty, and ethics played a role in his advancement?
- Has the candidate ever been placed under a significant amount of pressure (to meet individual or team performance goals) and responded by cutting corners, scapegoating, or deception?

You may have to talk to people who have worked with the candidate to receive accurate answers to these questions. If you do, be sure to talk to superiors, subordinates, and peers so that you receive a wide range of feedback.

Strategist

The ability to think strategically is an easily overlooked trait. At first glance strategic thinking may not seem to fit with the alliance champion job. After all, doesn't the champion take the strategic lead from management? Isn't this at most a secondary trait rather than a primary one?

One of the most common reasons for alliances to fail is that they are created for short-term tactical reasons rather than long-term strategic ones. We've seen relationship managers who had only a vague idea about their company's market strengths, distribution objectives, or five-year plan. We've seen alliances founder because relationship managers didn't understand how to shape the alliance's goals to fit their organizational strategy. Management becomes frustrated when the alliance fails to help move that strategy forward.

It's not necessary that champions be on a company's strategic planning committee, but the company should have a mechanism in place to brief champions about anything that has an impact on strategic direction. Sometimes, however, the people managing alliances just don't have the temperament or experience to think strategically. This doesn't just sabotage Power of Two alliances; it can also prevent them from being formed in the first place, as the following story demonstrates.

Jim was a hard-charging sales executive responsible for all his company's collaborative efforts. He was terrific at extolling his company's product strengths—it was the leader in a number of markets—and did a good job of attracting prospective partners. One of those partners seemed to be an ideal fit for Jim's organization; there were numerous synergies between the two companies. The other company was ready to enter into an alliance. Jim made his pitch for the partnership at a meeting with his management, and he explained how the company's strong market share in key areas as well as its unique services would make the match a productive one.

What Jim didn't articulate—what he wasn't capable of articulating—was how the match worked from a strategic standpoint. He had never conducted a gap analysis and evaluated what the organization needed to reach its business targets; he rarely projected scenarios beyond the immediate quarter. As a result Jim couldn't make his argument for an alliance in purely strategic terms. All he could do was speak enthusiastically about what a great organization Company X was and how it possessed strengths his own company lacked.

Management turned Jim's proposal down and missed out on a potential Power of Two alliance. Two or three people on the management committee later confided that they felt Jim's motivation to forge the alliance was personal, that because he could only talk in terms of strengths and increased profitability they believed Jim wanted the alliance only for its short-term revenue-producing possibilities (Jim's compensation was tied to revenue produced by alliances he helped form).

How do you distinguish a short-term person like Jim from a true strategist? Look for someone who displays the following:

- Knowledge of the organization beyond his or her function
- A grasp of where the organization is heading three, four, or five years from now
- A willingness to invest time and resources in a project that may not pay dividends for months or even years
- Awareness of what the company is missing (in terms of technology, people, finances, and the like) that's preventing it from reaching its business objectives
- The ability to articulate a value proposition clearly and convincingly

Visionary

As we've emphasized, Power of Two alliances are different from other alliances in that they're not purely deal-making vehicles or ways to pounce on a hot market. Many times, Power of Two collaborations are established as part of a larger infrastructure network that will coalesce in anticipation of some future opportunity.

It takes vision to see a future market or trend that others can't see. It takes courage to express this vision and make a commitment to it.

Champions have this visionary zeal. It's nothing magical; they don't predict the future. But they are able to make a leap of imagination based on logical business analysis. They're skilled at constructing "what-if" scenarios: What if there's a downturn in the economy and our major competitor is bought and a new technology is brought in? Then X might happen. Some people do this naturally. Others use tools such as the one found in Peter Schwartz's book *The Art of the Long View* (Doubleday, 1991). He talks about how he and his colleagues at Global Business Network develop three or four possible future scenarios for corporations, factoring in political, social, and technical environments.

For instance, many organizations are concerned about the future impact of the Internet on their businesses. To construct scenarios, they might formulate a question such as, What impact will the Internet have on my business in the future and what other companies should I align with today to be prepared to address this potential market opportunity?

The next step is to identify the driving forces for this scenario. One might be the speed with which business adopts the technology necessary to make Internet sales a reality. Another driving force might involve the issue of an open market—is it dominated by a few service providers or is it wide open? Using these forces, you can create three or four scenarios. Then you can decide which business partner makes the most sense for your organization given each scenario, and which ones make sense given the gap between what your company is today and what it must be to take advantage of the scenario tomorrow.

Power of Two alliances seem like they have crystal balls. Competitors wonder how an alliance managed to position itself with the right people and resources years before an opportunity broke. The legerdemain of alliance champions is a result of their willingness to craft and explore scenarios. They've formed alliances that put them in a great position not only for Scenario A but for Scenarios B, C, and D.

Visionaries are always in great demand and short supply. How do you unearth them for your champion positions? The following five-step process might help:

1. Identify people who are good at coming up with different alternatives and possibilities; they will probably also be good at constructing alternative scenarios.

2. Eliminate people who are pie-in-the-sky visionaries, who base their visions on nothing more than whims and wishes.

3. Look for individuals who do their homework first and craft their visions later—they do the pedestrian research and data-base analysis at the start of the process and their visions emerge from what they've learned.

4. Separate the people who think ahead in the singular from those who think ahead in the plural. Some managers are great at looking at how customer product requirements might change and have an impact on their function—that's the sin-gular. Others are skilled at looking at how they might have an impact on a group of functions and companies—that's the plural. Visionaries are proficient at projecting the impact of an event on numerous parties; they can conceive of how an infra-structure network of many companies might be put together to take advantage of a scenario.

5. Look for people who can eloquently state their vision. Not everyone can communicate a vision powerfully, but this is often a requirement of champions, who must generate support for a given scenario from their management group and their allies.

Planner

When companies collaborate, planning is often missing from the equation. Typically an alliance begins work by staffing up, dividing the market, giving each relationship manager a set of numerical and MBO goals, and putting a compensation plan in place to support desired short-term behaviors. If there's a larger plan, it usually in-volves some variation on the theme of "getting more business."

If your champion is not a planner, then the odds are you won't get more business because the alliance won't last long enough. Con-sider this case:

A large athletic shoe manufacturer entered into an alliance with a very successful sports agenting firm. The relationship manager for the shoe company had a simple get-more-business plan in his head. He carried it out by recruiting a number of top salespeople and telling them to meet all the agents they could and convince them that they should work together to gain endorsements, tournament sponsorships, and joint advertising promotions. Certainly these were appropriate goals, but they weren't achievable given the lack of planning. The salespeople did meet many agents—and this resulted in many promising reports to the shoe company's senior management—but no deals were struck during the first six months of the alliance. Not only had senior management's expectations been raised but they'd invested a significant amount of money and people in the alliance without any return.

Senior management put pressure on the relationship manager for results, and the relationship manager put pressure on his salespeople. The salespeople, in turn, put pressure on their agent contacts, who resented what they felt were high-pressure tactics not in keeping with the spirit of the alliance. In less than a year, the alliance was dissolved.

Champions start the alliance off with a plan, making sure the champion at the partner company is involved in shaping it. They set expectations for the alliance for each of the first five years. During the planning, it may turn out that it's unrealistic to expect a return on investment until the third year. If senior management from either partner views this schedule as unacceptable, it's important to get that on the table from the start. Either the plan has to be adjusted in a realistic way or there's no point in continuing.

The champion who is an expert planner can help sidestep a common alliance pitfall. We've seen many companies enter into an alliance with a bang (though not a plan), and within a year decide they've made a bad choice in partners. They end that alliance and enter into a new one, repeating this pattern so frequently that they might go through five partners in five years with nothing to show for their efforts.

Power of Two alliances are rooted in a plan, and the champion is adept at putting one together (in conjunction with the champion from the alliance partner). The champion uses the plan in a number of ways, including these:

- To help determine the value proposition for the two prospective allies to work together
- To identify any potential barriers that might prevent that value from being realized
- To gain buy-in for the alliance from senior management and different business units
- To avoid surprises that might occur if everyone hadn't signed off on the plan

We can't overemphasize how important a planning mind-set is for champions. Power of Two alliances need to be strong in order to survive, especially if the alliance is between two dissimilar competitors or organizations. Alliances are weakened when the allies are working under different assumptions about when results will be achieved or what those results should be. Plans spell these things out. When the alliance goes according to plan during that first year, it builds confidence and trust and strengthens the alliance.

We'll talk about how to put together a Power of Two plan later, but it's important for you to understand what a champion needs to address when formulating one. A champion requires a fairly wide breadth and depth of knowledge to create a plan, because it addresses such diverse issues as these:

- *Value proposition*—the win-win scenario of the alliance; why a given market will respond to your product or service if you partner
- *Barriers*—what or who might prevent you from realizing the value proposition
- *Objectives*—for years one through five, the specific business objectives the alliance needs to achieve

- *Tactics*—the specific business development efforts required from the alliance to achieve the objectives

Champions insist on specificity in planning rather than vagueness. We've found that when plans are filled with generalities and uncertain language, alliances falter. Commitments need to be made—who will do what when. Champions insist that these commitments be made in writing in advance of the alliance launch.

When searching your organization for people who are natural planners, determine if they do the following:

- Favor specifics over generalities
- Create effective reports, strategies, and recommendations by working with others as opposed to working alone
- Consistently meet deadlines and achieve goals
- Are realistic in their expectations rather than pie-in-the-sky dreamers
- Are good at projecting possibilities and alternatives instead of seeing only one possible scenario

Communicator

A champion must be able to get his ideas across clearly and concisely to people who might not "speak his language." An alliance partner comes from a different organization with different policies, procedures, and culture. Modes of communication in Company A may be the opposite of Company B; for example, A may favor a great deal of electronic communication whereas B relies on the old-fashioned medium of paper. Or A may emphasize open and direct dialogue but B still has a number of protocols about the type of questions that can be asked and how they can be asked.

Champions transcend these differences. They're comfortable talking to anyone in their own company and in their partner's. They can talk to large groups and are also effective one-on-one.

They're especially talented at helping people understand complex propositions. Alliances can involve intricate issues that aren't immediately grasped. For instance, it's not always easy for alliance members to recognize the benefits of partnering to capitalize on an opportunity in a new and different market. Champions can bring these opportunities to life; they have the knack of making hypothetical scenarios immediate and real. They don't get sidetracked when explaining and convincing; they cut to the heart of the matter.

Finding great communicators within your organization can be done by looking for people with the ability to do the following:

- Interact equally well with top executives and the rank-and-file
- Synthesize a variety of opinions and ideas and explain them simply and powerfully
- Speak in a way that makes the listener feel as if his or her response counts
- Help teams of diverse people understand their mission
- Persuade people to do things they express initial reluctance about doing

Collaborator

When we mention this trait, some people jump to the conclusion that we're really referring to negotiation—that to collaborate well with a partner means negotiating a beneficial working arrangement. Though there may be a need for some negotiation in Power of Two alliances, champions don't need to be expert negotiators. In fact, some good negotiators make bad champions. They have a tendency to demand things from partners, to beg, threaten, and push hard to get what their organization wants.

Power of Two alliances require champions who look at collaboration as win-win propositions. Actually, they look at them as win-win-win scenarios, the third winner being the existing or prospective customer. They see the value of long-term relationships and work hard at making sure everyone involved in the alliance benefits. Negotiators, however, focus on the short-term win and don't worry about long-term consequences.

Good collaborators are often good facilitators. In Power of Two alliances, champions adroitly move information and ideas back and forth. Instead of being merely receptive to new concepts, they solicit them. Champions take a proactive stance, understanding that a constant exchange of ideas is critical for healthy collaborative efforts. They don't rely on existing systems to facilitate this change. In some instances, a company or its partner (or both) is saddled with secretive cultures, slow approval processes, and other factors that make true collaboration problematic. Champions find ways to bypass these problems.

Champions aren't "empty" collaborators. Some people collaborate for collaboration's sake, unconcerned if an alliance produces anything of value. Alliance champions work to ensure that collaborations count for something. Many meetings between relationship managers, for instance, accomplish nothing because they don't understand how to collaborate productively. Champions frequently start meetings by setting forth objectives and asking for consensus on them. This tactic clearly communicates that the point of the meeting isn't simply to talk but to accomplish significant goals.

In searching for people with this skill, it's important to separate negotiators from collaborators. To see if you can, place an N or C next to each of these descriptions of people:

1. Is a talented deal maker, willing to work overtime to make sure an issue is settled

2. Has a background in business development and knows instinctively what to give up in order to get something

3. Focuses on making sure that all parties leave a room feeling as if their goals were met

4. Sees the implications and ramifications of decisions and factors them into the process

5. Is willing to use any tactic necessary to keep a partnership on track and moving toward its objective

6. Reacts to an exciting new idea or piece of information by sharing it with someone else rather than hoarding it

Answers: 1N, 2N, 3C, 4C, 5N, 6C.

Persistence

In a champion, persistence is more than mere stubbornness. It grows out of a sincere and deep belief in what an alliance stands for and in its ultimate goals. This belief fuels the champion's persistence no matter how many setbacks and roadblocks occur. Consider this case:

> Nina is a champion who works for a mid-sized company in the medical products field that began teaming with a health care research institution. In the past their markets had been different, but changes in technology and other conditions demonstrated that they each had something to gain by focusing on the other's markets.
>
> Both organizations began the alliance tentatively. After about a year, however, both groups became excited about an opportunity and agreed to pursue it together. The agreement called for Nina's company to provide the expertise and services while the other company provided the funding and products. Everything was moving forward smoothly until the eleventh hour, when the other company abruptly decided it couldn't afford the investment and pulled out of the project. Nina received a great deal of flack from management, which wanted to know how this could have happened and whether the alliance should end.
>
> Nina too was upset with the company's partner, though she had a better understanding of the financial difficulties that prompted its surprising pullout. Nina also felt that despite this setback the factors that pulled the two companies together in the first place were still viable. Based on a year of working with the other company she was

convinced that the fit was good and that there would be other projects that would have happier endings—if they could hold the alliance together.

After a great deal of effort on Nina's part—she met privately a number of times with the CEO and CFO and lobbied hard for them to support the alliance—they went forward with a small project and it turned out well. Within the next two years they partnered on three major initiatives that helped both companies gain footholds in each other's markets.

In some Power of Two alliances it may take two or three botched efforts before the alliance enjoys success. People from both companies may snipe or even attempt to sabotage the partnership. Champions are lightning rods for criticism, and they can't take it personally or become enmeshed in vitriolic arguments about who is to blame when things don't work out as expected. Most of all, they need to support the alliance if they believe it's still worthwhile. Because the big opportunities for the alliance might not flower for months or even years, champions need to keep alliances alive and well until then. That takes persistence, and not everyone has that quality.

We've found that persistent people often exhibit the following behaviors:

- They support an idea they believe in even if it's not politically expedient or they're not in the majority.

- They push for a project consistently even if they've been turned down more than once. They're not obnoxious about it, but they keep proposing it until they get a chance to move forward.

- Their persistence is logical and flexible; they push for something only as long as they believe in it, and they're willing to change and adapt their ideas if it gives them a better chance of succeeding.

- They weather criticism and questions well; they don't give up just because a superior expresses skepticism or scorn for their idea.

- They're focused. They don't flit from project to project, leaving one behind because a newer and better one appears; they're good at concentrating their efforts in support of the concept or recommendation that strikes them as most important.

Getting the Best People to Apply for the Job

We would be remiss if we concluded our discussion of the champion without noting that it can be a tough position to fill. Many alliances draw their relationship managers from the ranks of sales and marketing, and it's true these people tend to have an affinity for developing relationships and a sizable number of contacts. Though these are good attributes for champions, they are by no means the only ones, as this chapter illustrates. Unfortunately, management may not look beyond the marketing and sales department for people to drive alliances, and even within that department may be unwilling to choose the best people for the job—it'd rather have them generating revenue than managing an alliance.

Another issue is motivation. From the perspective of any one employee interested in the position, the recognition for being champion often seems slight. Most companies don't offer significant financial compensation for alliance champions. They also don't offer access to resources or prestige within the organization.

As a result, in many companies the best people aren't seeking the role of alliance champion. This needs to change, and we believe it will change as organizations recognize how important alliances are to their future. When they comprehend that forming and managing Power of Two alliances are the keys to that future, the recognition for champions will change accordingly and attract people who are qualified for this cutting-edge job.

We believe, going into the next century, that the alliance champion will play as significant, if not more significant, a role in the strategy of a company as that of the chief information officer. In the 1980s, companies realized that the use of information could provide a competitive advantage. They raised the level of the information technology manager to that of strategist and corporate officer. The same will occur with the alliance champion when companies realize the role the Power of Two alliance will play in their strategy.

Chapter Six

Alliance Analysis

A paradox of Power of Two alliances is the need to be both open-minded and discriminating when considering prospective partners. As pointed out in Chapter Two, it is a mistake to partner with prejudice and avoid certain types of companies and alliances. Still, you need to be selective in choosing from your leveraged network.

We've found that alliance analysis rarely occurs on a meaningful level. Too often, the only analysis that is done revolves around one key factor. For instance, companies choose partners based on financial criteria: Does Company ABC have the resources necessary to help us make a short-term profit? In the rush to market, alliances ignore all other factors. Shared values and beliefs are frequently overlooked as criteria. It's no wonder that many alliances founder when its members discover that their methods of operation, ethics, and expectations are diametrically opposed. Blinded by what seemed to be a perfect match, both partners fail to examine these other issues when putting the alliance together.

It takes a bit of time for organizations to determine if they are a good Power of Two match. But it's time well spent, as the following example attests.

The Power of Patience

Two organizations were considering an alliance—let's call them Smallserve (for small service firm) and Bigco (for big corporation). They were initially attracted by each other's strengths: Smallserve had pioneered a number of highly innovative service concepts and

Bigco possessed a state-of-the-art product line. It struck both organizations that if they combined their distinct yet complimentary strengths they might open some exciting customer doors that had been closed to them in the past.

As part of the same leveraged network, they had some familiarity with each other. But they were much more familiar with some of the other network members and therefore decided not to rush forward. Though Bigco's president was anxious to achieve additional growth in the current fiscal year, he had recently appointed an alliance champion who insisted that the company get to know Smallserve before going further. At the Bigco champion's urging, Smallserve appointed its own champion from within its ranks and the two began exchanging information and ideas. They shared everything from their histories to their cultures and goals. They provided each other with references from others in their network so each of them could receive unbiased commentary from people they trusted. The two champions met regularly, reporting back to their organizations about what they had learned. Everyone agreed that the two companies were well matched in critical areas and that they should form an alliance.

It took six months for this final decision to be made. Certainly there was some grumbling in management ranks that a great deal of time and energy had been spent on this so-called alliance without a nickel of profit to show for it. But that grumbling stopped a bit later when a customer emerged who needed the synergistic mix of skills this Power of Two alliance offered. A presentation was made and the alliance won the business. Its performance on the account was outstanding—the customer couldn't believe that this was the first time they had worked together, noting that "it seems like you guys have worked together forever." Within the next eighteen months the alliance won seven additional pieces of business, all stemming from its great performance on the first job.

If this had been a traditional partnership, it probably would have been dissolved early on. If the two companies had concentrated only on a fast financial return, the alliance wouldn't have lasted. It's quite possible that the alliance might have secured a customer before that six-month learning period if it had aggressively pursued prospects and not bothered to learn from and about each other. But it's also likely that its performance would have suffered. The point of analyzing a prospective alliance isn't just to be sure that the two companies are compatible on all fronts; it's also to provide familiarity with business practices and to identify potential disconnects and dissonance. Anticipating problems before they occur and taking steps to prevent them are hallmarks of Power of Two relationships.

The Criteria

Ten Factors to Consider Before Formalizing the Relationship

To a certain extent, alliance analysis is more art than science. Champions are especially adept at sensing a prospective alliance partner's compatibility. They have almost a sixth sense for all the intangibles that go into making a solid Power of Two alliance. After working with another champion for a while they know if their cultures will blend, if they share the same ethical standards, if there are synergies just waiting to be unleashed. Choose the right champion and you'll increase the odds that you'll analyze a potential alliance partner properly.

At the same time, you can't just rely on a champion's intuition. A number of concrete issues must be analyzed critically and thoroughly before committing to an alliance. Over the years, we've compiled ten criteria for Power of Two alliances. These criteria often evolved out of mistakes we've witnessed and made in forming and managing alliances. Certainly these aren't the only things to consider before entering into an alliance; you may find that there are other, "customized" issues you need to consider before moving forward. You'll want to evaluate your current alliances and relationships against these criteria also. Just because an alliance is in place doesn't mean it's a good one or that it is based on sound principles and expectations. In the Power of Two alliance one must be ready to terminate an alliance that's not working. Don't let it drag on until there are bitter feelings about resources wasted and opportunities missed. Keep in mind that the goal of Power of Two alliances focuses on long-term opportunities, not short-term deals.

Before introducing the ten criteria, we want to caution you against assigning a potential alliance partner a numerical rating—in other words, ranking a company "5" because it meets five out of the ten criteria. Such a ranking is misleading for a number of reasons, not the least of which is that some of the criteria might not be relevant for a given company. For example, Company A may have great products and support, which is the value proposition that you seek from it, but may lack marketing capabilities. That may not be important if you are relying on another source—perhaps someone in your leveraged network—for marketing support.

If you start assigning numbers, adding up the score, and analyzing data, you may get the wrong picture of the value of the relationship. At least you'll get the wrong picture from a Power of Two alliance perspective. The Power of Two alliance focuses on the people and relationships that make it work, and the personal and professional relationships you have with your alliance partner cannot be measured by numbers. The goal here, then, is to provide you with a subjective measurement of issues that have been important to Power of Two alliances we've been associated with. The criteria for these alliances follow:

1. State of the alliance partner's business and driving forces

2. Market presence

3. Alliance readiness

4. Product and service quality

5. Sales and customer support

6. Problem-solving approach

7. Financial considerations

8. Knowledge-sharing ability
9. Marketing
10. Flexibility

The following offers questions designed to elicit the information you need for each point. Some of the information you can obtain from web sites, annual reports, customers, other leveraged network partners, executives at the potential alliance partner, and others that you have relationships with in the company.

1. *State of the Alliance Partner's Business and Driving Forces*

In this category you want to understand the general financial health of the company, including these factors:

- Annual sales revenue
- Profitability
- Annual growth
- Expenditures on research and training
- Experience of the people in the company

You also want to ask the following questions:

Is quality, growth or profitability the company's driving force?

How is it organized: central or distributed?

How does it make decisions?

Is it a solution company, a product company, or a service company?

Are the people running the organization talented and visionary leaders?

The key here is to figure out not only if the company is financially stable but if its focus and direction coincides with the opportunities you're looking for. You may discover that a company makes decisions unilaterally—that one person acts as a virtual dictator when it comes to important choices. Power of Two alliances don't function well when one of the partners operates under a dictatorship. You may also discover that a potential partner is focused on improving its product quality whereas you're pursuing growth strategies. Though these two goals aren't necessarily incompatible, they may be, and it makes sense to do some additional homework.

What you're looking for here (and in the other criteria) are disconnects as well as synergies. Where does the fit seem perfect? Where do you seem ill-matched? In answering these questions, be careful when you assess a prospect's financial figures, especially if they're much smaller or larger than your own. As we've emphasized earlier, the size of the potential ally is not important, just the experience and skills of the people running it. Big companies can be run by small-minded people and small companies by big-picture thinkers. Figure out if the leadership harmonizes with yours, not if the revenue figures match up.

2. Market Presence

Answering the following questions will give you a sense of the company's current strategy:

> Where does it sell? North America? Asia-Pacific?
> What industries does it sell to?
> What is its market share?
> What references does it have?
> How does it bring its product or service to market? With a direct sales force, a manufacturer's rep, distributors, mail order, electronic commerce via the Web, or alliance partners?

Determine not only where the company is today but envision where it could be as part of an alliance with your company or your competition. Brainstorm some scenarios by asking questions such as these:

Where does the other company's market strengths offset your weaknesses? Where might its weaknesses cause you problems because of your lack of strength in that area?

In what geographical area or industry might you pursue an opportunity together? Where doesn't it make sense to work together?

Can you conceive of how your combined resources might enable the alliance to create a new market, become a leader in a market, or create a strong niche?

3. Alliance Readiness

You can't assume a company will make a great alliance partner because it has extensive experience with alliances. Nor can you assume that just because a company is part of your network a Power of Two alliance will naturally evolve. Some companies are ready for the Power of Two challenge and others aren't. To determine which is which, consider the following questions:

Has the potential partner entered into partnership, alliances, and collaborations in the past? What were the results?

Is teaming part of its culture? Part of the culture of its sales organization? Marketing group? Engineering people? Product development function?

Is the executive team supportive of alliances?

Does the company team with its competitors?

Is it willing to share risk?

Are there any competitive or regulatory restrictions to partnering?

Does it have an alliance infrastructure in place with formal contracts, support groups, and processes?

Is it part of your leveraged network?

Ironically, organizations with a strong internal alliance history and structure may not make the best Power of Two partners. Some may have established alliance rules and agendas that are antithetical to Power of Two alliances. They may also have experienced alliance failures that cause management to be overly cautious about who they partner with and how. Others do well in an alliance despite a lack of experience, such as one we coached:

> A medium-sized service company had no experience with alliances but realized that if it were to grow it needed to pursue opportunities with larger corporations. For that it needed an alliance partner in order to learn the skills and resources required for this step and to help round out its portfolio of services. The management team had very little experience with forming or managing alliances but was very open to our coaching. The company's culture was based on customer service. It appointed a vice president of operations to be the champion of alliances. This organization was alliance-ready even though it was new to the practice. It had the right attitude and commitment.

4. Product and Service Quality

Let's start out with a simple rule of thumb: don't form alliances with organizations that have significantly different standards of product and service quality. If you do, your joint customers will let you know about it, probably dooming the alliance in the process. We've seen many companies enter into alliances assuming that their partner shares the same product and service quality standards. Sometimes they rely on reputation and publicity rather than doing any serious investigation. And sometimes this issue just doesn't seem to elicit much concern, the logic being that if one partner has great quality it will overcome whatever defects the other partner is saddled with.

If you're best in class, however, you better be sure that your ally has a similar standing. Your current and new customers will judge you based on how your alliance performs, and we've seen instances where one company's poor performance in product and service areas has harmed the other company's customer relationships.

To avoid this problem, ask these questions:

Is the potential ally one of the top three in its category (assuming that you're one of the top three in your category)?

Are its service offerings as flexible as yours?

Does it offer the same type of industry standard warranty as you do?

Does it operate under product quality manufacturing standards that are similar to yours?

How does it rate in terms of service speed, efficiency, and innovation?

Does it have a track record for solid R&D?

5. Sales and Customer Support

This is an even less tangible topic than product and service quality. Organizations often have highly idiosyncratic approaches to sales and customer service. Their approach may be effective for them, but it may be totally unacceptable to you (and to your customers). A company is often shocked when its partner will not do whatever is necessary to win a piece of business, or dismayed when it makes little more than a token effort to create top-notch sales proposals, product demonstrations, and presentations.

One of the most obvious ways to judge the feasibility of an alliance—and one of the most frequently overlooked—is to discuss the potential partner with your customers. What do they know about the company? Have they ever worked with it? Would they like to? Do they believe it's a good match for you? One organization we worked with hired an independent consultant to do this research. It was planning on forming an alliance with a competitor, which would require a significant expenditure of money and time. An independent consultant was used for two reasons: first, to verify what the champion had concluded through his research, that the competitor would make a good alliance partner in the consumer package goods marketplace; and second, so that the champion could use the consultant's report to allay the fears of his executive team about the ability of the competitor to deliver what it said it could to customers and to respond to those people in the organization who felt the competitor was not trustworthy. As it turned out, the competitor had an excellent relationship with its customers. This would not be likely if it typically cut corners.

Here are some additional questions to ask and actions to take:

Talk to the potential partner's customers. Are they satisfied with you as a partner? Do they believe you match up well?

Investigate its sales procedures and policies. Does it install its products? Does it have twenty-four-hour response capability? How does it support global customers?

Determine the company's willingness to compromise and change. For instance, is it willing to customize its products and services to meet the needs of your customers?

Discuss with a potential partner how you might approach joint prospects. Would it be willing to provide evaluation copies of its product? Would it defer to your lead in creating the presentation in certain situations?

Does it have the resources and the willingness to support proposal development, demonstration development, benchmark studies?

What is the reputation of its sales force?

Does it improve your ability to deliver global solutions?

If you see an unusual theme in some of these questions, you're starting to think in Power of Two terms. They are designed to determine if a partner will be flexible, open, ethical, and exploratory in its sales efforts. Power of Two alliances require this free-flowing mind-set here and elsewhere.

6. Problem-Solving Approach

Alliances can break up when problems arise, especially if one partner is shocked to see how the other responds to problems. Some cultures encourage seat-of-the-pants solutions. Others have formal processes in place for dealing with very specific types of problems and insist those processes be used. As a result, you enjoy a viable alliance until a customer starts complaining or some other problem arises. In the example discussed earlier, the company knew exactly how the competitor addressed problems with its customers:

> A product manufacturing company and a small product company teamed with a small service company that had a leading-edge solution. The product company shipped a prototype product to their first joint customer. It wasn't until the second week that the customer and the small service company started having problems with the prototype. They called the local support representatives from the product manufacturer. The support people could not provide a lot of help because the product was new. They didn't escalate the problem but tried to deal with it by calling the factory for help.
>
> After two weeks the customer got quite angry and told the service company that if the problem wasn't fixed in days it would cancel the order. The champion of the service company was finally brought into the discussion; he called the vice president of manufacturing at the product manufacturing company because he had a business relationship with her. She responded by sending a new machine and one of her engineers to the customer site. The service company champion knew that she would respond, based on his experience with her in other situations. His next call was to the relationship manager at the product manufacturing company to find out why he had not provided a plan to support the new prototype; this had put the customer and the alliance at risk.

Power of Two allies understand in advance how they'll confront problems when they arise. A consensus on problem solving is usually much easier to achieve when both companies have compatible problem-solving styles and plan for crises up front. To determine if this is the case, ask the following questions:

> Does the company have a process in place to address customer complaints, returns, and the like? How similar is that process to your own?
>
> What types of major problems has the company encountered in the past and how has it dealt with them?
>
> If you and your partner were to have a problem while working together, what do you feel would be the best way to resolve it? What does your partner feel would be the best resolution?

7. *Financial Considerations*

Certainly most partnerships begin with a common understanding of financial goals. In the old business paradigm, companies rarely moved forward without discussing what each wanted to get out of the alliance. In the Power of Two paradigm, however, financial considerations must be understood on a deeper level. That means spelling out in detail how much the alliance will invest annually, how the budget might be changed, and how the money generated will be divided (revenue sharing, commissions, independent contractors who collect revenue separately, or other methods).

But another aspect of finances must be taken into account by Power of Two partners. Because you're not doing a deal in the traditional sense of the term you may not realize a financial gain from the alliance immediately. It's also possible that the gain will be indirect rather than direct—you'll profit by the knowledge you receive or by the new opportunities that come your way.

The following questions and actions should facilitate a deeper and more wide-ranging analysis of financial issues:

> How soon do you and your partner expect or need to see some financial results from the alliance?

Is your partner as excited about the potential knowledge-
sharing opportunities the alliance will generate as about the
financial gain?

How much is your partner willing to invest in the alliance in
terms of dollars, people, and resources?

How willing is this company to change its investment in or
financial goals for the alliance based on changing circumstances and opportunities?

Benchmark the proposed financial arrangement against those
created between other alliances (this helps ensure that the
arrangement is fair and no one feels cheated).

Document the arrangement in writing to avoid the misunderstandings that come from purely verbal agreements.

Set up a measurement device to determine if the alliance is
meeting the expected financial objectives.

8. *Knowledge Sharing*

Everyone gives lip service to this concept, but it can often be a
source of friction in business relationships. In Power of Two alliances, knowledge sharing is a cornerstone of the relationship. In
some instances it's the point of the relationship. For companies
stuck in the old paradigm, this is a difficult concept to grasp. These
companies consider certain areas to be off-limits—not only to outsiders but to many insiders as well.

When push comes to shove—when allies are called upon to
share financial or market data—problems often result. Misunderstandings about what information may be exchanged can easily destroy alliances. To prevent this from happening, you and your
prospective Power of Two ally should address the following questions:

Will you provide each other with information about product
strategies, finances, marketing strategies, benchmarking results, proprietary research, and the like?

Will this exchange of information be open and continual or will there be certain restrictions and time frames placed upon it?

How will information be exchanged? Will it be verbally, on paper, electronically, or by some combination of the three? Will an existing Intranet system be used or will one be created?

Will each party allow the other to attend its internal training courses?

Is each willing to share information about its customer base?

We have seen more and more companies open up their internal employee training to their alliance partners. Their rationale is that these partners are an extension of their organization who thus need to know as much about their products as their own employees if they are to present them to customers or do R&D to enhance them. (In the old paradigm, some of these same companies would not think to let outsiders into their internal training. There were company secrets to protect.) We have participated in some of these internal training sessions in which management delivered a strong message to its own employees that alliance partners were important to the company. The fact that we were there made it a stronger message.

9. Marketing

This can be a dicey issue, especially when one partner feels that the other is taking advantage of an alliance to achieve selfish objectives. For instance, we've seen companies use an alliance with a larger, better-known organization in order to take advantage of their distribution networks, to get publicity, and to gain knowledge about a market. None of this is intrinsically wrong, but Power of Two allies have an understanding from the beginning about each partner's goals in a variety of areas, including and especially marketing.

Here are some questions that will yield useful data about your partner's marketing intentions and willingness to market the alliance itself:

Does the potential partner have a specific marketing objective that it is depending on the alliance to help meet?

Is it weak from a marketing standpoint and in great need of assistance in this area?

Will you create joint advertising?

Will you work together to produce alliance public relations?

Is there a need for and will you create an alliance brochure?

What will be your budget for promoting the alliance? Will it be split equally?

Will you attend industry trade shows together? Will you create a booth for these shows?

Will the other company deliver presentations and papers at industry conferences with you?

Will it allow you to use its name in your marketing presentations and advertising? Will you allow it to use yours?

Is the company willing to share leads that it develops independently?

10. Flexibility

Expect the unexpected—that's wise advice for Power of Two allies. As much as you try to discuss and document issues raised by the previous criteria, you're bound to be thrown a curve by the marketplace. In a rapidly changing world, it's virtually impossible to anticipate and plan for every opportunity or problem that might present itself. Therefore flexibility is important, and both allies should talk about how flexible they're willing to be. You also need to assess your willingness to share risk.

Analyzing your partner's flexibility (not to mention your own) isn't easy. You and your partner may pledge to be flexible now but find that you become more rigid as financial and other pressures limit your options later on. Still, you should at least analyze the factors that have an impact on a company's flexibility:

Has your partner ever changed a business strategy in midstream? Has it done so with a product introduction, in the area of customer service, with an advertising campaign, with a new corporate policy? When something has gone wrong, has it been able to switch gears quickly?

Ask the same questions of yourself and determine whether you are more, less, or about the same as your potential partner in terms of flexibility.

What would happen if an opportunity you never expected arises that is outside the boundaries of what you came together to pursue? Would your partner be willing to pursue it? Would you? What might prevent either of you from pursuing it?

Would you and your partner be willing to invest more resources in order to pursue an unexpected opportunity?

Would you change your pricing in order to secure a high-potential customer?

Would you continue the alliance even if none of the expected opportunities are realized in the first year of the relationship?

Evolving Criteria

Don't measure a partner against these criteria once and forget the results. We advocate using the questions in this chapter again and again. See how a company measures up not only before you enter a relationship but at various times after the relationship has been formed. It may be that an ally learns from you and becomes much more flexible as the alliance develops. It's possible it will feel much more comfortable about sharing knowledge a few months into the alliance than at its inception. Or vice versa.

Our point is that Power of Two alliances recognize that things change, including the alliances themselves. By getting a reading early on and comparing and contrasting later analyses, you put yourself in a good position to figure out where the alliance is heading. You can also compare your prealliance findings against alliance realities—was your initial analysis of a company's suitability as a partner correct?

Using the criteria set forth in this chapter over time will help you refine them. You may learn that it's important to give more weight to one criterion over others; you may choose to add, subtract, or change questions that you use in your analysis. The key is to develop the best analytical tool possible so that you choose an alliance partner worthy of being a Power of Two ally.

Chapter Seven

Cocreating Business Opportunities

Opportunities take many forms. They may include everything from expanding into new markets to growing your business to going global. It may involve dealing with an upcoming governmental initiative, an environmental imperative, or an emerging customer need. Power of Two alliances view opportunities holistically. They recognize that the opportunity isn't always one that leads to short-term profit. Power of Two alliances understand that great opportunities exist for discovering fresh ideas or new knowledge, and that the opportunity might be in an unfamiliar or untraditional area.

Some of you may have extensive experience in working with other organizations to cocreate opportunities. Some of you may have only created opportunities on your own. Most of you will be unfamiliar with the Power of Two approach to opportunity generation. As you'll discover, it's an approach built on trust, flexibility, and quality rather than profit, power, and quantity.

The First One with the Most Alliances Does Not Win

Although the Power of Two approach mandates an open-minded attitude toward partners, it does not advocate an open-door policy. Not any partner will do. In fact, many companies out there couldn't cocreate an opportunity in a million years. We suspect that many CEOs and other top executives recognize the importance of making a qualitative match, of finding a partner that can provide a synergistic mix of ideas and resources. They probably also understand that it's important to establish a partnership with someone who understands the gestalt of partnering and values relationship building.

This recognition often gets lost in the rush to team. Partnering is hot, and companies often end up partnering at a fast and furious clip. The typical scenario goes like this. A company decides that alliances are now a strategic part of its business strategy and hires someone from inside or outside the company to be vice president of business partners, general manager of business development, or director of alliances. Our experience has shown that this person (or the staff of people the person hires) immediately begins calling other companies and offers the following proposition: "My company wants to have an alliance with you; who do I need to talk to in order to get this done?"

Wrong! If you follow this course of action you'll probably end up with an administrator, a contracts person, or a marketing person who has responsibility for signing up alliance partners. People in these positions are often measured on how many alliance partners they sign up. They are provided with no motivation or training in leveraging the relationship with alliance partners to achieve the goals of the business unit (which is why Power of Two alliance champions are aligned with the business unit).

We've seen an alarming number of companies that are focused on signing up alliance partners. They crank out press releases on a regular basis announcing another alliance as if the mere merging of resources guarantees a positive outcome. When a company starts by telling you one of its value propositions is the number of alliances it has, consider yourself warned. You should also avoid this acquisitive strategy. Quite a few companies in the technology sector are realizing the downside of this strategy. They went through the sign-everyone-up stage and discovered that many allies didn't help them attain their business unit goals. They also discovered that maintaining all of these alliance relationships was very expensive. Technology companies are now reducing the number of partnering relationships they have; they're also raising the qualifications for admittance to their alliance partner programs.

When you're looking for a prospective Power of Two ally who will help you cocreate incredible opportunities, keep the following rules in mind:

1. Quantity is no substitute for quality; be selective and don't move forward at breakneck speed.

2. Establish a relationship with someone who values relationships (ideally this will be someone with the title of alliance champion) and not with an administrator or salesperson.

3. Look for an organization that has a track record of delivering value to customers; it may be better able to deliver value to the alliance in the form of opportunities.

The Only Thing Alliance Programs Create Is More Mail

It's very difficult to cocreate opportunities as part of an anonymous, sprawling alliance. Nonetheless, we know organizations are tempted to join these programs and capitalize on the promise of alliances. You should be aware of what happens when you join these programs. First, you're added to a mailing list and likely will become overwhelmed with your new alliance partner's company and product literature. Your company's name gets added to that company's list of alliance partners, which then gets mailed to their other alliance partners. There's also a good chance your company's name will get posted on its web site.

If you want unqualified exposure, that's what you'll get with this type of program. Our experience has been that you will get unqualified phone calls from people who want to know everything from your hourly rate for services to your list and discount prices for products. They will want copies of company literature or solicit you to join other alliance programs. For the alliance neophyte, the activity level often suggests a false sense of progress. You believe that your network is growing. All this activity will take your focus off what you are really trying to accomplish through an alliance: to cocreate opportunities.

Preparing to Pursue an Opportunity

Ideally, Power of Two partners emerge from an established alliance network. Someone within that network approaches you about an opportunity (or you approach someone in that network). Ideally, you already know a bit, or it's easy to find out, about your prospective partner. Even if a prospective partner isn't in or connected to your network in some way, you need to discover something about its value proposition and how that meshes (or clashes) with your value proposition. Does the opportunity satisfy both propositions?

In our eagerness not to let an opportunity slip away, we sometimes forge alliances first and ask questions later. Here's an example:

A sizable venture capital firm approached a small but quickly growing alternative medicine company about partnering to develop a new vitamin in response to studies that showed the health benefits of green tea. The alternative medicine company didn't hesitate for a moment; it figured if it didn't partner with the venture capital firm, the firm would simply partner with a competitor. Had it done a bit of homework, however, it would have found that this venture capital firm had a history of approaching companies with partnership ideas as a way to do market research. The firm would milk its "partners" for all the information they possessed and then reevaluate the original opportunity. Many times it would either decide the opportunity wasn't worth pursuing or decide it needed new partners who could better capitalize on the opportunity. In this instance, the alternative medicine company had done a considerable amount of research when the venture capital firm decided the costs of developing a product were too high and the market too small for them to move forward.

Before jumping into alliances to capitalize on opportunities, ask the following two general questions:

1. What type of alliance history does my prospective partner have? Has it left behind a trail of dissatisfied or satisfied partners?
2. Does the opportunity under discussion meet the partner's value proposition as well as ours?

From there, proceed to specific questions that give both you and your partner some specifics to talk about. We've found that many partnering discussions avoid critical details necessary to assess an opportunity realistically. Sometimes this is because companies haven't done their homework. Other times there's a reluctance to get into the nitty-gritty aspects of an opportunity until a partnering agreement has been reached. Power of Two alliances, however, begin from a strong knowledge base. We suggest answering the following questions to develop that base:

1. What is the opportunity?
2. What types of resources are needed to take full advantage of the opportunity?
3. Who are all the people or organizations that could be involved with the opportunity?
4. What steps need to be taken to initiate this opportunity?
5. What roadblocks might exist to slow down or stop the creation of this opportunity?
6. What creative solutions can you come up with to address these roadblocks?

New business opportunities may have the following goals:

• To launch a new product
• To pursue a new market segment

- To create a new technology
- To pool resources to leverage both organizations
- To generate new ideas
- To generate a new service offering
- To share business practices
- To gain access to new expertise
- To open up new geographic territories
- To exchange knowledge capital

Once you and a prospective partner have agreed on a mutual goal, the next step is to determine if this partner is in the best position to supply the resources you lack in order to capitalize on the opportunity. As we detailed in our earlier alliance analysis chapter, your partner will help you fill the gaps between what you have and what you're missing relative to an opportunity.

Move forward cautiously. The vast majority of opportunities will still be there when you wake up the next morning. Qualify a prospective partner's interest. Instead of forming an alliance to go after an opportunity during your first meeting, talk about the possibility of a "teaming" or "collaborative" initiative. It's expensive and time-consuming to form an alliance; it's also psychologically detrimental to form one only to find that it's not viable shortly thereafter.

Power of Two alliances often don't really coalesce until after two companies have partnered successfully on two, three, or more small opportunities. These provisional alliances test the waters, giving both partners an idea if they should invest more time, money, and effort to pursue bigger opportunities. Though it's not necessary to follow this path, it often allows a Power of Two alliance to evolve slowly and naturally rather than be thrown together without adequate preparation.

Let's say you decide you want to partner with a company to go after a small opportunity. To help move the alliance toward Power of Two status, it's important for you to suggest that your partner appoint a champion (if it doesn't already have one). Don't be shy about recommending someone in its organization as champion or about expressing your reservations about someone who you feel is a poor candidate for the job.

Once you both have champions in place you can talk about some of the core issues that come with the pursuit of any opportunity. Some of these are sensitive subjects, and alliance champions are best able to handle these subjects with equanimity. Some questions you might want to ask each other include these:

Will anyone in the organization be hurt if you go after an opportunity together? Might any political sensibilities be offended? Will the alliance tread on someone's territory?

How will you support each other in pursuit of the opportunity? Can one organization provide training that might be helpful?

How is the reward system set up in each company for achieving alliance goals? If the alliance capitalizes on the opportunity, who benefits and how? Are the rewards clear, motivating, and relatively equal in both organizations?

Dealing with these questions not only facilitates work on opportunities but helps develop the alliance infrastructure. The more each partner knows about the other—the more familiar each becomes with the other's policies and procedures—the better able the alliance will be to pursue future opportunities together. The alliance infrastructure is constructed out of an exchange of knowledge, and the more that is known the stronger the infrastructure will be.

All over the Map

Brainstorming, or what is commonly called a "mapping" exercise, is often used to create the awareness of what each alliance partner brings to the table for partnering. However, our experience has been that the mapping of products and services by the marketing groups of both organizations is premature and wastes time. When this map gets to the respective field, sales, or business units organizations it is usually discarded because it was not based on the real capabilities of the delivery organizations but rather on the perceived capabilities of the respective marketing organizations or the executive teams. Here's a case in point:

> Several years ago a major technology company decided to team up with a large consulting firm to attack the retail banking marketplace. The manager of the service organization in each company shared a vision of how both companies could bring a strong value proposition to the market with a new product and a set of services delivered by each company. They developed the product based on their experience. Just as the product was about to be released, they did a mapping exercise that stated the technology company would do the network services, the technology services around the products, and the maintenance services. The consulting company would do the strategic planning and project management.
>
> When the first real business opportunity was identified, the corporate marketing people faxed out the map of services and responsibilities. The local technology company's sales team rejected the map outright. They "owned" the relationship with the customer and therefore wanted to determine the role the consultant would play. When they found out that the map had not been based on any real experiences between the two organizations, the map lost credibility altogether. The champions for both organizations got involved in negotiating a teaming relationship between the respective field organizations trying to use the map as a guide, but found that many of the assumptions made by the corporate marketing groups were wrong. The champions were involved in the next half dozen opportunities, negotiating the teaming infrastructure. Each time they used the past teaming agreements as references with the field teams, not the map from headquarters.

Another problem with mapping the capabilities of each organization at the headquarters level is that you may come to the con-

clusion that there is no opportunity for each organization to leverage the other. This is especially true when you are trying to bring
traditional competitors to the same table. The consulting firm just
mentioned recently went through another mapping exercise with a
computer company. (Apparently it learned little from the first experience.) The resulting map concluded that the two organizations
were head-on competitors with no room for cooperation. Mean-
while, however, the champions of the two were executing teaming
agreements between their respective field organizations for specific
business opportunities. The field organizations understood that they
were competitors but that they needed to meet the demands of
their customers. They created new opportunities by packaging a
total product and service offering that encouraged their customers
to move forward because the alliance team was mitigating risk for
them through their alliance partnership.

Whenever alliance partners are considering a new opportunity,
we suggest they consider the "three Cs" of alliances:

- Competitiveness—people and resources
- Capability—skills and products
- Capacity—relationships with customers, suppliers, and other
  influencers

A company's capacity, capability, or ability to compete given a new
opportunity may vary by time, geography, or market. If your company lacks one of the three Cs, that's the time to consider engaging
an alliance partner.

The consulting firm may not have the technical skills (capability), people (capacity), or customer relationship (competitiveness)
for a given situation, but its alliance partner might; thus it could be
prudent to team up.

In general, we feel that the mapping exercise should not be
done up front when you are discussing a teaming relationship,
though it could be part of the alliance discussion further down the
road when you have more experience to base it on. As consultants,

we will not participate in one of these exercises during the initial discussion stage. Clients are often disappointed at this because they see the map as a clear deliverable that they can show to their organization to demonstrate that they are making progress, but it is important to focus on those activities that help the alliance progress.

Cocreating with Confidence

Once both champions have been designated, the next step is to create widespread alignment within the alliance about opportunities. Organizations are complex organisms, and for alliances to be effective they can't be treated as simple, one-cell entities. As the alliance cocreates opportunities, issues will arise that reverberate throughout the organization. When one company brings the other an opportunity to invest in a new technology, a manufacturing executive may feel his turf is being invaded. When the alliance decides to go after a market in a foreign country, the international people may rebel. Opportunities may bring out cross-functional feuds, simmering political squabbles, and the conflicting agendas of local business units and corporate offices. Opportunities can easily be squandered if champions fail to address key issues before the opportunities are pursued.

One of the best ways is to get a sense of how people in both organizations view collaborative efforts. Do they have much experience with teaming? Have there been problems in this area in the past? Who caused those problems? How do organizations measure the success of a given venture? Are there different measurements based on who is doing the measuring?

A big problem we've seen is that one partner in an alliance goes after opportunities with a set profitability goal in mind. They don't view a new piece of knowledge, the chance to explore a new market, or testing exciting technologies as an adequate reward. Many times management in such a company recognizes the value of these goals but business unit heads don't. That's why champions should determine if a given opportunity might not meet a profitability goal and take steps to avoid resistance.

One of the easiest ways to avoid this resistance is by obtaining buy-in from senior management before meeting with a partner's local business unit. We've seen local business unit heads discover during an alliance meeting that an opportunity won't lead to the financial windfall they expected and immediately opt out of the opportunity. Many times they'll say all the right things during the meeting and won't explicitly state that they've lost interest in the opportunity. But when the alliance needs their support, ideas, or energy, it doesn't receive it.

As two new partners focus on an opportunity for the first time, they're walking on eggshells. To make it through this fragile period intact, Power of Two alliances do the following:

Make Small Commitments.   These commitments can take many forms. It may be an exchange of white papers on an opportunity-related subject, sharing technical information, offering partners drafts of teaming agreements that have been used successfully in the past, or bringing a top executive to a meeting. These are acts of good faith that give both partners the confidence to keep moving forward.

Get the Champions Involved.   Do this not just from a headquarters level but in the field. Problems are inevitable as alliances start working on opportunities. Feelings are hurt, toes get stepped on. Champions need to be where the hurt is; they need to keep everyone focused on the opportunity rather than let them get distracted by relationship issues. Champions set priorities, obtain resources, and do everything possible to move the alliance closer to its opportunity goals. Once those goals are achieved, everyone breathes easier and the alliance has a real-world basis for confidence.

Facilitate Sharing of Sensitive Information.   Sign a nondisclosure agreement to facilitate the sharing of sensitive information. This may not seem like a good symbol of a trusting alliance, but it provides reassurance to many people throughout both organizations. Although champions may trust each other, various executives in both companies may be skeptical about revealing strategic and financial information to outsiders, or they may not grasp the Power of Two alliance concept. Nondisclosure agreements provide a measure of reassurance. Reassurance also comes from referring to past teaming successes. When you can provide a current partner with a case history that illustrates the benefits of sharing information, it · greatly facilitates this process.

Confidence comes from personal collaboration. We've found that some alliances attempt to cocreate opportunities electronically. They rely on faxes, Intranet exchanges, phone calls, and e-mail to move forward. But Power of Two alliances thrive on the energy and excitement generated by a roomful of people who share common goals. It helps a lot to see your collaborators in person, to hear their voices, to observe their body language. We could get some argument on this point, but it's difficult to know someone electronically.

In addition, our experience shows that alliances become sidetracked without regular personal contact. It's much easier to iron out differences face to face rather than modem to modem. For example, when two companies decide to develop a product together there are stated and unstated arguments about which company has the better product development process, manufacturing technologies, materials, and so on. Though these arguments certainly can flare in personal interactions, they usually can be resolved quickly and smoothly through intelligent discussion. When working electronically, people waste enormous amounts of time sending lots of documents attempting to prove their points.

More, Better, and Unexpected Opportunities

Traditional alliances often form to pursue traditional opportunities. One or both companies spot an emerging trend or hot market and they join forces to take advantage of it. They follow a straight, familiar line from seeing the opportunity to capitalizing on it.

Power of Two alliances may also follow a straight line, but more often than not they zig and zag. The energy, creativity, and flexibility of Power of Two alliances often leads them in unexpected directions. Two companies may come together to explore the possibility of opening offices in the Pacific Rim and discover that they can better accomplish their goals by opening additional offices in the American southwest.

The opportunities Power of Two partners cocreate often are the result of a knowledge exchange, of trading information and ideas that uncover new possibilities. Here's an example:

> Companies A and B had partnered to export a line of products to Latin America. As they moved toward that goal they communicated regularly. They shared research, conducted focus groups together, held a series of brainstorming sessions, sent each other articles from trade publications, and held a series of meetings. At one of these meetings, the champion from Company A and a relationship manager from Company B were discussing their alliance opportunities in the United States when manager B mentioned that his company was planning on doing a lot of hiring in Latin America over the next year to support new opportunities in the financial services market. Champion A realized his company had the resources to support that effort, as it had opened an office in Mexico City a year earlier that could handle more business. Shortly thereafter, Company B agreed to accept Company A's human resources support, and its expansion proceeded smoothly. Recognizing the potential people synergies, the alliance began supporting each other in other endeavors. What had started as an alliance designed to take advantage of product opportunities turned into one focused on people opportunities.

Information exchanges in Power of Two alliances are value-added. People don't just go through the motions; meaningful ideas and relevant data are exchanged. And they're exchanged in all sorts of ways through all sorts of interactions. As important as meetings, written correspondence, and phone calls are, there are other options you should consider:

- Jointly presenting a paper at industry conferences
- Going to trade shows together
- Jointly publicizing products and services
- Linking virtually to one another via the Internet
- Conducting a research study together
- Benchmarking another company's process or best practices
- Visiting a current customer (of one of the companies in the alliance) or a prospective customer

These different environments supercharge the knowledge exchange. They present partners with contexts and situations that push them to rely on each other in different ways and to look at problems and solutions in a fresh light. This sets the stage for the cocreation of extraordinary opportunities.

Chapter Eight

Rules of Engagement

You've analyzed a number of potential partners and have finally decided on one. You both agree to go forward, and each of you is understandably excited about the alliance's potential. In the euphoria of the moment, however, you may overlook a crucial step—a step necessary for any Power of Two alliance.

Before you move forward, the Power of Two philosophy defines how each organization will engage with the other to obtain the objectives of the alliance and to pursue specific business opportunities. If you don't set rules—or, worse, if the partners operate by different, unstated rules—then the alliance will never reach the potential you and your partner envisioned. The rules of engagement provide structure for the alliance to take risks, be innovative, and explore opportunities flexibly and imaginatively. With rules in place, both alliance partners feel more confident—they aren't operating only on a wing and a prayer. At the same time, the rules provide guidance when the alliance pursues an opportunity. In many instances, such pursuit takes the alliance in unexpected directions. Disagreements and other forms of conflict are common when an alliance partnership explores new territory: Do we go faster or slower? Do we spend more or less? Rules assist alliance partners in making these decisions and help manage the conflict that can arise.

Rules of engagement don't just tell the alliance what it should do but what it shouldn't do. Every alliance needs to set limits—lines the alliance cannot cross—and the time to do this is at the beginning of the partnership.

We've created the following rules based on our experiences with many different alliances. There may be many other rules, but we've focused on a handful—just five:

- Define roles and responsibilities
- Put an escalation process in place
- Implement a communications plan
- Create and deliver a solid customer proposal
- Ensure successful delivery of your solution

Though you may modify these according to your particular circumstances, they should work well for any type of Power of Two alliance. It may seem like a lot of work, and maybe even unnecessary based on your experience, but two good champions can put most of this together in a day or two. Like any good planning effort, the more effort you put into your rules of engagement up front, the less time will be spent by the champions resolving disputes.

Define Roles and Responsibilities

This is the key to setting realistic expectations and eliminating false ones. When the parties involved never discuss what their respective roles and responsibilities will be, alliances fail. We know of an alliance between a large manufacturing company and a small product innovation firm that floundered because of a lack of role definition. Going in, the product firm assumed that it would come up with the ideas for products and the manufacturer would provide the resources and dollars to produce them. Actually the manufacturer wanted a major say in creating ideas and also figured that the product innovation people should share the financial risk. Had all this been clarified at the beginning, the alliance may not have failed. Even when conflict broke out over this issue, the problem wasn't that the product innovation company was unwilling to share in the risk, but that it felt misled (as did the manufacturing company). In reality, neither intentionally misled the other. They just never voiced their agenda out loud for the other to hear. Bad blood caused by missed expectations led to the break, not the issues, which might have been negotiated away.

As we've discussed before, missed expectations of what each organization is going to get out of the alliance often leads to its death. Just as critical are expectations of what each will put in to the alliance. You need to define where the alliance is applicable and where it doesn't work. This is particularly important when you are forming an alliance with a competitor. The alliances we have worked with that involved competitors are the ones that drove us to defining roles, responsibilities, and an escalation process.

Following are some of the common role and responsibility categories that should be defined from the very beginning:

- Financial (who will invest how much when; under what circumstances the investment formula might change)
- Resources (technology and human; what hard and soft skills Company A will provide versus Company B)
- Time (how many hours both partners will devote to the alliance in field work, meetings, presentations, and the like)
- Key people (who from each organization will be point people on the alliance team)
- Boundaries for the alliance (markets, geography, size of opportunities, and the like; no alliance can be positioned as all things to all the organizations involved)

Defining roles and responsibilities is important when you and your alliance partner pursue a business opportunity. It is also necessary when you want to maintain a productive relationship with a partner when there is no immediate financial profit from the alliance.

If the objective of the alliance is knowledge exchange between two organizations, then the people to drive the exchange must be identified and some objectives set. How often will the exchange happen, and by what means? Will you meet quarterly? Will there be a monthly conference call, weekly video conference, or daily electronic communications? Who will meet, who will set it up and prepare the agenda, who will take the meeting minutes? Will there be a private web site to communicate? Who will build and maintain it? Who will fund it? In a knowledge exchange relationship, if you have decided together to share your findings with the marketplace, then what conferences will you do it at? Or perhaps you will hold your own conference. One organization we worked with brought together a number of its alliance partners to annual think-tank retreats where they showcased leading consultants and speakers to address the issues they felt most pressing. These value-added events help develop personal trust among the participants, who share their concerns and interests in their individual and group development. We've seen manager after manager walk away from these sessions with better-defined plans for creating joint profit initiatives.

As you can see from these questions, it might be easy to sign an alliance to share knowledge about the marketplace, or about each other's or a competitor's product developments, but still fail because you did not define the roles and responsibilities of each partner. The same can be said for a joint research relationship that focuses on products or services. Maintaining a solid alliance partnership based on knowledge or research requires as much focus and attention as one based on a business opportunity.

We also suggest that roles and responsibilities be formalized in writing. This might strike you as a throwback to the old deal-making paradigm where neither partner trusted the other. It also might seem to contradict the Power of Two reliance on personal relationships between champions where one's word is one's bond. Writing out roles and responsibilities, however, is not the same as insisting on a legal contract that details financial arrangements between partners. The objective here is not to use a legal document to ensure compliance with a verbal agreement, but simply to avoid the miscommunication and false assumptions that emerge in a world of change and complexity. Both parties can enter the alliance with the best of intentions but still fall victim to a confusing, evolving marketplace. Here's an example:

> A service company and a product company put together an alliance to pursue the communication services market. At many meetings between the executives, each talked about their core capabilities and where they were already strong in the marketplace. The goal of the alliance was to get stronger together in markets where they had little presence. There was always a relationship manager (but not a champion) present at these meetings, many of which occurred over lunch or dinner so there weren't always good meeting notes to document the discussions and agreements. The executives had agreements in principle on how training, sales support, product development, and market development would occur. They signed the legal documents and began marketing their joint, state-of-the-art product and service offering.
>
> Suddenly they had five new opportunities to sell and deliver their joint solution. The respective sales and service organizations got together and that's when the conflicts began. The relationship managers of each organization began refereeing who would take the lead on the proposals, who would provide the demonstration products, who would talk to the prospects, and on and on. The service and product company did win quite a few of these opportunities but they were painful for all involved. It took longer to win the business and longer to install the solutions. Meanwhile, technology in the market started to change. The window of opportunity eventually closed for this alliance. The respective companies didn't have to resolve it, the marketplace did it for them.

Putting roles and responsibilities on paper is especially important when you're working with people rooted in other cultures, industries, or countries. Here are two other compelling reasons to put it down in writing:

- Talk is cheap. As the alliance is being forged, people are caught up in the excitement of the moment. We've seen people proclaim they'd "make sure our best people are working on this alliance project" or "commit all our resources to achieve the alliance goals." Writing these role statements down tends to make people think about what they're really willing to do for the alliance.

- People are increasingly transitory. You may forge an alliance agreement with Mary, but before you know it she's been removed from her role as champion or has left the company. There's often a significant gap between starting the alliance and pursuing a real business opportunity. During that time, key people in the alliance can disappear. If roles and responsibilities are documented, then a new champion can step in and take over where the other left off.

Put an Escalation Process in Place

Champions anticipate that there will be problems between alliance partners and that other levels of executives will need to be involved in resolving these problems. There will be differences over the strategy necessary to pursue a business opportunity, who is responsible for a particular action item, or how expenses will be shared. You may need to deal with individuals in either company who don't support your alliance strategy. What do you do when you find yourself working with people whose principles and resulting actions don't support the values of the alliance?

Having a plan that anticipates how you will resolve these disputes through intervention of multiple levels of management provides at least two benefits. First, it gains more meaningful commitments from the management team of both organizations to work with each other on the business opportunity being considered; and second, it secures a commitment from both management teams to act as the mediators for any disputes.

The escalation plan should be put in place after the alliance is agreed to but before you begin to pursue the objectives of the alliance or a joint business opportunity. You want to set up the alliance environment so that disputes are resolved immediately. If the alliance champions or project managers understand up front that their failure to come to an understanding on the issues will be escalated up to their respective management teams—and if they understand when that might happen—damage will be minimized when an impasse occurs.

Without an escalation plan, one champion may feel the other champion is going over his head to talk to senior management about a problem. We've seen champions and relationship managers react defensively when this occurs, feeling that their alliance partner doesn't trust them to do the right thing. Even worse, they believe you've made them look bad in front of their organization. As a result of all this, they dig in harder and cease trying to work with you to solve the problem; all their energies are directed to defensive reaction. They may say they're trying to do what's right for their organization, which unfortunately may not be what's right for the alliance. Consider this case:

A product manufacturing company agreed to work with a service company at a financial services institution. The two had agreed on their respective roles. It was fairly simple: the manufacturer provided the product and expertise and the service company installed the products at the customer site. This was a very big project for the customer with a lot of visibility at executive management. So when a number of delays cropped up, the service company expected an immediate response from the manufacturer's local team. When it didn't get that, the service company called the manufacturer's vice president of sales—not the relationship manager or regional manager—to voice a complaint. This got an immediate response, of course; the manufacturer couldn't afford to lose such a large opportunity.

After the same thing happened a couple of times, the manufacturer's relationship manager arranged for his regional manager to meet with the service company's project manager for breakfast every Monday morning to review the project's progress. As a result, the regional manager and the services project manager developed a good working relationship. The calls for assistance didn't go to the vice president any more. The local team of the manufacturing company responded quickly and provided better service to its alliance partner and the financial services customer.

Yet both the local team and the regional manager frequently complained to the manufacturer's relationship manager that they didn't trust or even like the service company people because of the way the latter chose to escalate problems. This bitter feeling didn't go away. Eventually the alliance at that customer broke up; two years later the manufacturing products company was able to replace the services company to serve that customer.

If the relationship managers had been Power of Two alliance champions, they would have anticipated having problems with such a big project and would have put an escalation plan in place. They could have included themselves in the escalation chain so that they could keep a handle on the issues, help develop a relationship between the local teams of the product and service companies, and ensure a basis for future work together.

Implement a Communications Plan

Two food product companies teamed up to capitalize on what they believed would be a growing institutional market. With Company A's technological resources and Company B's base of institutional customers, they were sure they could capitalize on emerging opportunities. One of Company B's customers had just purchased another organization and was now in a position to provide cafeteria service to hundreds of colleges across the country. Company A's champion, as soon as he heard of the deal, was on the phone to the customer pitching the alliance's capabilities (he'd been introduced to the customer by Company B's champion at a social event). When Company B's champion heard about this pitch, however, he was furious. He thought they had an understanding that they would approach his organization's customers as a team, never independently. Though the champion from Company B apologized, the alliance relationship took a step back as the champions had to patch their relationship and define how communications would occur in the future.

Putting an alliance communications plan in place and following it is an essential rule of engagement. It's especially important for all interactions with customers, both present and prospective. Who is allowed to talk to each company's customers? How should they be approached? Who should serve as the alliance contact with the customer? How should they make formal and informal presentations? These and other questions need to be discussed before an opportunity arises, not when it's happening. You must plan your communications so that you present a united front to the customer. When a customer senses that each ally is looking out for its own interests, then the customer has difficulty trusting the alliance. When customers sense a lack of cohesion in the alliance, they're naturally concerned that it won't hold together for long.

The Power of Two alliance enables a network of relationships to consider many opportunities with many different partners. This strategy offers many benefits but also some challenges. It may be difficult to keep track of who you are partnering with and who you are competing with on any given initiative. All the alliance partners must actively declare their intentions. Up front you must discuss whether you are teaming together, acting as independent contractors, or competing. Sometimes when an opportunity to work together is identified it is not clear what the best strategy will be for each organization. It is up to the champions to keep communications open until the alliance partnering decision has been made. Then it should be documented in a letter so there will be no misunderstandings. Here's a case that further illustrates why this is so:

Many years ago it was not uncommon for consulting organizations in what were then the Big Eight accounting firms to talk to many technology companies about teaming on specific business opportunities. An inexperienced relationship manager at one technology company set up a meeting with one of the Big Eight to discuss teaming on a $10 million opportunity. The sales manager of the technology company made a bad assumption: that the presence of the Big Eight firm at the meeting meant its commitment to team. He shared information about his product strategy for the opportunity, which he deemed confidential. Two days later the sales manager found out that the Big Eight firm had teamed with one of his competitors to bid on the opportunity. Naturally, he was livid. He went to his relationship manager to complain; when the relationship manager investigated, his counterpart at the Big Eight firm told him that the firm had had meetings with four technology companies that week to determine who was the best fit to bid with it on the business opportunity. It was standard business practice; there was no intent to deceive anyone.

If the relationship manager had communicated up front the objective of the meeting he'd called and the status of each company with respect to an alliance, this misunderstanding would have been avoided. The sales manager wouldn't have been so open with his information—or, if he had, it would have been with his eyes wide open.

To establish effective alliance communications, you need the following in your plan:

- Alliance team communication to the prospective customer
- Communication within your own organization
- Communication between alliance partners

The plan needs to identify who is responsible for communicating with whom and to establish some do's and don'ts. These things don't have to be rigid or overly specific; they do need to establish some parameters within which the alliance can communicate effectively. For example, it might be perfectly all right for engineers in both allied companies to have ongoing conversations without the participation of the champions or some project leader. Or maybe not: some project managers want to be part of all communications because they feel a need to ensure that all commitments made by the parties are kept and that they are within the scope of the alliance. It depends on style. By setting the framework and getting buy-in from all involved parties, communication breakdowns can be avoided.

We were once involved in the following knowledge-sharing relationship:

A software tools company and a software application company entered an alliance to design and build their respective products to be compatible with each other and to drive the standards of the industry. The products weren't to be released for sale for at least nine months and it would take another nine to twelve months to establish themselves as a leader in the industry. It was important, though, to keep the development moving to get to the market before anyone else. The executives and the champions outlined the objectives for the alliance with some time frames. At the initial meeting, the management team agreed to meet once a quarter to review the progress of the development initiatives, develop marketing strategy, and identify early business opportunities. If any issue arose between their organizations that the champions could not resolve, the team would handle it via a conference call that could be put together within a week. At this meeting, the team designated a contact in each engineering group and authorized these individuals to communicate on a regular basis with each other and to use the champions to address business issues. This alliance has worked out very well. A couple of times, the engineering organization of one company fell behind in development, which in turn had an impact on the efforts of the other. But whenever it looked like the alliance was losing steam, it was put back on track by the executive team at its quarterly meetings.

The team reset expectations, reassigned engineering leads, and appropriated resources as necessary at these meetings. A couple of times the champions set up conference calls to avert crises. The planned communication and commitment by the management team kept this alliance focused on the end objective.

One issue to highlight in a good communications plan is the requirement that no one withhold any information that is important to the alliance. Each partner also needs to inform the other of any potential change in the alliance. For example, if a potential customer suggests to one partner that it would be better off teaming up with another organization, that partner needs to let its ally know what the customer is thinking. The ramifications on the overall alliance of terminating the teaming arrangement for this particular customer should also be discussed, as should the possibility of approaching the customer jointly and making a case for keeping the team intact.

Consider this case:

Many years ago two very large organizations, a service company (Company X) and a service-product company (Company Y), had a teaming agreement. They had signed a written agreement to make a proposal for a multinational telecommunications solution. They informed the customer of their intention. The customer told Company Y it would prefer that Company Y teamed up with a service company other than Company X—the chance of being awarded the business would be better. Company Y sat on this information while it thought about the ramifications of dumping Company X or of telling the customer that it wouldn't do so. Besides not telling the Company X business unit manager what was going on, Company Y did not tell the relationship managers either. But the business unit manager eventually found out what was going on from another source. He was furious that his alliance partner had not shared the customer's misgivings about Company X with him. The teaming opportunity broke up, so did the overall alliance, and the Company X business unit manager would have nothing to do with Company Y for years.

In this case, Company Y broke trust by not sharing essential information. The relationship managers were at fault here for not setting up clear points of contact for communications and for not detailing to all parties what critical information needed to be shared between the alliance partners. Sometimes it just has to be said to all parties: to build and maintain trust, you must communicate all information that has an impact on the alliance, good or bad.

Unclear communications within an organization can be a roadblock to the continuing development of an alliance. Review another case:

Two service companies had been doing business together for two years. They were very successful, and so decided to expand the alliance to include another service of one of the companies. They agreed on the business arrangement, documented it, and drafted a contract to support the new arrangement. Company A had escalated the new arrangement to its senior management for approval and informed other divisions within the organization of its intent to expand the alliance. Company B made certain to receive approval from its mid-level management but had not passed it by senior management for review. When senior management found out, it put a halt to the process until it could review the new offering and understand its implications. Not knowing about the new alliance initiative caused this problem, not the substance of the initiative itself. This was very embarrassing to the relationship manager from Company A; he'd been working on the deal for more than sixty days, and the problem delayed the whole contract signing and therefore the service offering for another thirty days. This meant lost business for both sides, but also lost credibility for Company A's relationship manager and for Company B—all because the relationship manager had not understood who had to be in the communications loop up front.

These issues are not uncommon. Anticipating their occurrence and mapping out communication strategies is something that Power of Two alliances always do. We will discuss the role of communications further in Chapter Ten.

Create and Deliver a Solid Customer Proposal

The reason for this is to demonstrate the potential power of the team. When an opportunity arises, the members of an alliance need to put their heads together and produce a viable proposal.

Proposals are a litmus test for alliances. We find that companies can become very sensitive when they realize that their name will be in a document or a presentation with their alliance partner, and these do reflect on the professionalism and capabilities of all parties involved. The key to success here is to keep focused on the deliverables for the customer, not on the methods, documents, or practices of any of the companies participating in the alliance. Simmering resentments, pride of ownership, and brewing conflicts can bubble to the surface under the heat of the proposal process. This heat can be reduced if champions have hammered out guidelines for putting proposals together and presenting them.

To deal with these issues, decide these matters in advance:

- Who will query the customer on clarifications of key points
- Who will lead the proposal effort
- Whether the proposal will be based on your standard terms and conditions, your partner's, or some combination
- Who will create and give presentations
- Who will demonstrate the solution
- Who will bear the cost of putting the proposal together and of the presentations and demonstrations
- Where the proposal will be put together (Will the proposal team share office space from the beginning as they work or will each partner work separately on sections and cobble them together later?)

- Whether the team will need to pilot the solution contained in the proposal

- Who will pay for the pilot and who will do the work (these can be shared equally or prorated based on a revenue-sharing arrangement)

- Who will do the research on competitors for a project or an account (unearthing the competitors' pricing, technology, and marketing strategies, whether they have alliance partners, whether they've teamed before, and the like)

While setting the rules for proposal making, the issue of references needs to be addressed. Customers may wonder if your alliance has worked together on a project before; they may want to know if you've ever teamed with other companies and, if so, whether you can provide references from those experiences. We've found that customers are wary of various forms of conflict between "allies"; they've been driven mad (and driven away from alliances) by partners who finger-point and bicker constantly.

Not too long ago we were at the presentation of an alliance proposal to a customer who asked, "Where have the two of you worked together before?" The alliance team was totally unprepared for the question. The members stumbled through an ad hoc response about how they had formed successful alliances with other companies in the past, but they apologized for not being able to name those companies because of confidentiality issues. As a result of their fumbling, the customer sensed that this team had not worked together before and had not worked out all the issues with respect to delivering a joint solution (the customer was right, by the way). The alliance team didn't put together a compelling enough story to address the prospective customer's fears, the customer didn't want to put its business in the hands of a team that wasn't a team yet, and so the alliance didn't get this piece of business. In fact, both companies had teamed successfully with other companies and they could have put together an impressive list of big-name customers who were more than satisfied with their efforts.

Even if you're forming an alliance with a given company for the first time, don't make a proposal without references. Expect a customer to question how the two of you will work together and formulate a cogent response. The following two cases illustrate the power of developing and following guidelines for presenting a prospective customer with a true joint proposal.

A government opportunity worth tens of millions of dollars was bid on by two service companies and a half dozen small product companies who had formed an alliance for this purpose. The executives from the service companies—one a technical service company, the other a consulting service company—originally met to test the waters and see if they could coexist on the same team. Could they split the services pie, so to speak? When they realized that neither had the resources to go after the opportunity alone, they agreed to team. An executive at each of the service companies assumed the champion roles.

The two companies signed a letter of understanding and later completed a detailed teaming agreement stating the roles of each. When the product companies joined later they signed teaming agreements also. The bulk of the risk for implementation of the solution would be borne by the service companies if they won the business. Thus the champions played a hands-on role in the beginning, when roles were being defined and resources committed. They each appointed project managers to lead the day-to-day task of managing the proposal effort and the pilot. The government agency required each bidder to propose its solution and pilot it for six months. The proposal and development effort alone would take eighteen months.

The champions decided up front that they would split the cost of the proposal effort 55–45; that was the revenue-sharing split they would receive if they won the business. This split only applied to out-of-pocket costs. When the team of eighty people from the two organizations was housed in some empty space in one of the technical service company's buildings, for example, it was not included in the shared expenses because there was no incremental cost to the technical service company. The printing of the proposal was a shared expense.

Every time a dispute arose between the project managers over who was responsible for a portion of the proposal development or the associated cost, they referred to the teaming agreement that documented roles and responsibilities. If it was unclear they escalated to the champions, who interpreted the agreement within the spirit of their agreed-to relationship.

Another opportunity involved a service company and a manufacturing company that agreed to team to build a customer information system for a bank. The two had teamed together on other opportunities, but not very successfully; in a few cases they had barely made it out of the proposal stage. The reason was that they had not laid out a comprehensive plan for how to prepare a joint proposal for a client. They'd agreed to work in their own offices and fax pieces of the proposal back and forth for review and editing. The relationship manager would receive calls at home at night from both teams complaining about each other's style. "They're not doing it right!" was a common complaint, meaning: they're not doing it our way. They fought over format, over responsiveness, and over many other things. Each organization's culture was different, and communicating by phone wasn't helping either understand the other.

So, on the opportunity to build a customer information system for the bank, the relationship manager, who was now starting to think and act like a champion, convinced both organizations to locate the proposal team in the sales office of the manufacturing company. That was especially important given the circumstances: the team had not months but only a couple of weeks to find and propose the best solution. After the engineers and technicians determined the pieces of the solution, the proposal team locked itself in a conference room for three days to prepare the documents, with the champion having plenty of food sent in. The strategy worked; the members of the team spent so much time together, and so productively, that when the proposal was done they actually liked each other and went out to celebrate completing their task.

Ensure the Successful Delivery of Your Solution

The next step to your successful alliance teaming arrangement is the successful delivery of what you have jointly sold. Today's customer, if delivery goes well, will give a good reference to a prospective customer or to another potential partner in a future alliance.

At the delivery stage, all the talk is over, all the documentation is complete, and now it's time to carry out the alliance's promises. Power of Two alliances have a process in place to ensure that what the alliance promised is delivered. They don't just go at it by relying on seat-of-the-pants inspiration to see them through. Here is a process we've found to be effective for alliances we've worked with:

Project Manager. Identify this individual as soon as possible. The team of companies that have won the business must select one company to take the lead on delivering the solution; it could be a different one than led the proposal effort or made the presentation to the customer. Most alliance partners decide this when they agree to team on the business opportunity. From that company comes what we call the lead project manager, who will manage the resources of the team, ensuring that the team delivers what it promised and interfacing with the key customer contacts. To be successful with the customer, you can have only one lead project manager.

Each alliance partner needs to have its own project manager as well to ensure its commitments are met. Note that, depending on the size of the business opportunity and the resources required, this may not have to be a person's only responsibility. The point is that someone has to be on point in each company to make commitments, acquire resources, and escalate to management or the champion if someone or some group within the company is reluctant to help with the delivery.

You may say this is common sense, so why position it as a rule of engagement? We were involved in a teaming arrangement that demonstrates why:

> A product company and a services company had teamed up to win a significant contract to install a manufacturing system in a very large electronics corporation. The project was highly visible within the customer's organization because the new system would have great impact on its bottom line. The product company had the lead responsibility, as it had nurtured and developed the opportunity with the customer for years and had a good working relationship with its people. This relationship had served the alliance partners well in securing the contract but, looking back, it was not sufficient reason for the product company to lead the delivery; the service company, which had led many deliveries before, was better suited. But the product company felt it owned the relationship, insisted on leading the effort, and prevailed.
>
> Three months after the contract was awarded, the product company still had not appointed a lead project manager. Project dates were beginning to slip. When a project manager finally was named, he was not experienced in delivering a solution of this magnitude. Several months later, the customer itself stepped in and told the alliance that it wanted the service company to lead the project.

This example illustrates three points. First, the company that leads a project should do so because that is its core competency, not because it has a great relationship with the customer. Such a relationship helps make the sale and is important throughout the delivery of the solution, but it doesn't make the solution happen. Second, alliance partners need to be ready to appoint a lead project manager as soon as the customer awards them the business, or even beforehand if possible, so he or she can prepare the plan as detailed hereafter. Third, the lead project manager must be competent to lead a virtual team of individuals, to communicate effectively with all parties (including the customer) about the status of the project, and to escalate to management when necessary to obtain resources and commitments from all parties. We've found that this last point is the biggest challenge; some people on the project team will not be under the direct control of the lead project manager, so skill at influencing the entire team to pull together can be the difference between success and failure.

Project Plan. Create a project plan that will be the road map for all the alliance partners. This plan should be put together by the lead project manager with input from each alliance partner's project manager. Some things are particular to alliance project plans:

Identify the risks to the alliance and which alliance partners will assume the risk. For example, if a client wants one-second response for a new customer service computer system, and the alliance team agrees to build it that way but fails to achieve the goal, what do you do? Many alliances don't plan for such a problem. They assume everyone is going to be responsible for their part of the solution. When it doesn't work, the finger pointing usually starts. It could be that the computer hardware doesn't perform, or the software is defective, or the application developer did a bad job, or a little of each. You should decide up front who will bear the cost of fixing the problem. Will everyone share equally? Will it be prorated by how the revenue is being shared? Will it be the responsibility of the alliance partner deemed guilty by some criteria? In the example here, which was a real-life case, analysis determined that the computer hardware configuration was undersized. Though it had no plan for such a situation, the team agreed to share the costs of the fix because each party had been involved in planning the size of the system. The computer hardware company could have been deemed liable for the entire problem but was not. Instead, the computer system was upgraded, which fixed the response time to the customer's satisfaction, and the three companies came out of the experience wiser and committed to working with each other again. Which they did.

Identify any barriers or risks to the success of your team. These may be inside or outside the team's control. An example of a barrier outside the control of the alliance but within its influence is trade legislation. Say that an alliance moves forward assuming that trade will soon open up with a country in the Third World; it's planning on importing a product from a company there to be incorporated into its solution. But what if the legislation designed to open up trade isn't enacted? The alliance needs to anticipate that and have a course of action to find an alternate product. If there is no alternate source, the alliance partners need to weigh the consequences of withdrawing from the project if legislation fails to pass. Is it possible for the partners to influence the legislation?

A barrier to success within the control of the alliance might be the development of a software tool by one of the alliance partners. If it looks like the product will not be ready on time, is there a plan to put more resources on the project? Can the team find another alliance partner with a similar software tool? Should the project be delayed until the tool is ready? Should the alliance disband? A good project plan addresses these issues before they become issues.

Revise the escalation plan. Different people may need to be in the escalation loop for the development and delivery of a solution. Your escalation plan for developing the alliance and closing the business opportunity may have sales and executive management as the primary contact. The escalation plan for delivery of the solution may still include sales, but may also include engineering, operations, purchasing, legal, and other departments.

Implement a communications plan. It should focus on the delivery of the solution to the client. New members of the alliance team need to be briefed about who can talk to the customer, how information will be disseminated, and how they should communicate with others on the team. It is a good practice to call a team meeting of all the alliance partners to discuss the practices to be followed. Our experience has shown that this saves a lot of time later on. In some projects we have been involved with, communication to the alliance partners was a full-time job because the person doing it had to update each one individually instead of using a broadcast method such as e-mail. When you have commitments to keep, nothing is more frustrating than not knowing the next step. It leads members of the alliance to do things like call the customer to find out what's happening. As we mentioned earlier, this puts the customer in the communication loop for the alliance team.

Create a support plan for the customer. Sometimes alliance teams get so focused on delivering their solution on time and within budget that they forget to plan for ongoing customer support. Who will maintain that relationship and be concerned about customer satisfaction? Perhaps another alliance partner needs to be brought in to maintain the solution. Who will be responsible for updating the solution? What happens if the building burns down or the telecommunications or power is disrupted? What impact will that have on the customer's operations? The answers may determine when, or if, the alliance has further chances to do business with that customer.

Maintaining the Alliance: A Few "Don'ts"

Power of Two alliance partners never do certain things to each other; certain taboos must be observed by all if they want to preserve the special relationship they've created. Here are four "don'ts" that should be considered sacrosanct:

Don't let the customer get between you and your partner. A good communications plan will lessen the likelihood of this happening. It's not that a third party will intentionally try to break up the alliance. More likely it will simply make a request, look to get a more favorable arrangement, or suggest a strategy that better suits one partner's strengths—any of which may create a disagreement between partners. The key is to remember that if the Power of Two alliance is viable you'll be working with many different customers and pursuing many different opportunities. One customer should not be allowed to destroy or devalue that relationship.

Don't allow the alliance to become unbalanced. In other words, don't try to dominate the alliance or let yourself be dominated by your partner. If one party does start dominating discussions or pushing to have its way all the time, then you need to address the issue or use your escalation plan to resolve the conflict. Power of Two alliances draw their strength from the inherent equality of the alliance partnership, and it's up to both partners to maintain that equality.

Don't take your alliance partner for granted. When you've agreed with your partner to deliver a particular resource on a particular date, it's incumbent upon you to live up to that agreement. Power of Two allies don't make excuses to each other; they don't shirk responsibilities; they don't do things for each other only when it's convenient. More so than any other business relationship, the Power of Two alliance demands respect and reciprocity. If the original value proposition for the alliance is no longer evident, then end the alliance. When it's over, it's over. Don't let a withering alliance spoil the environment for another alliance in the future.

Don't withhold information. There will be times when you're hesitant about sharing data with an alliance partner, especially if it's a competitor. It may be sensitive financial information, research that you feel is proprietary, or information about a customer. Whatever it is, you violate a basic tenet of Power of Two alliances if you don't at least discuss with the champion at your alliance partner the nature of the information and the reason for your reluctance to share it. Champions trust each other implicitly. They recognize that their flexibility, speed, and creativity stems in large part from the free-flowing exchange of ideas and information between them. Withholding information does great damage to the relationship. If you can't trust the champion at your alliance partner, you have no business creating an alliance with that company.

The alliance champion should have at hand the five rules of engagement. They are a key value proposition of the alliance for whatever initiative or business opportunity it chooses to pursue.

The customer will appreciate having its success ensured by the alliance team having guidelines and processes in place. Executive management in the champion's company will like having rules in place to minimize risk for the company and its customers. Prospective alliance partners will view the champion and his company as well prepared to take on the challenges of an alliance and therefore as a good potential ally. Here are the rules again:

1. Define roles and responsibilities
2. Put an escalation process in place
3. Implement a communications plan
4. Create and deliver a solid customer proposal
5. Ensure successful delivery of your solution

Chapter Nine

Trust

The underlying basis of the Power of Two alliance is trust. Trust is desirable in any type of partnership, but essential for Power of Two relationships. Traditional alliances are cemented by other factors; sometimes one partner is so powerful that it can keep an alliance together through sheer force, sometimes two companies stick together because of greed or a clearly-defined goal.

In Power of Two alliances, however, the rules have changed. Goals may be amorphous and far off in the distance. Other times you're teaming with a competitor. The need to exchange sensitive information also changes the nature of the relationship. Trust is what holds everything together.

What Is Trust?

We view trust as a progressive initiative. By that we mean that it is something that flows through two alliance partnering organizations, starting with the champions. It's the champions' responsibility to develop trust within their own organizations—between and among all those who might influence the alliance. The phrase "building trust" is instructive. Champions literally must build trust in stages. They must move from one team sharing one piece of data toward multiple teams freely exchanging knowledge capital.

Trust must be built to the point that neither alliance partner questions the other's motives, refuses to share information, or feels the need to keep certain people within the alliance in the dark about various actions for fear they'll set up obstacles. It must be built until strategic direction can turn on a dime without arousing suspicions among allies about what proprietary interest is being served—and until the pursuit of an opportunity transcends all the politics and pettiness that crop up in any alliance partnership.

All this is easier said than done. Even for the most enlightened organizations trust is rare. In many companies we find a lot of lip service given to trust. We hear the term bandied about in many ways: "You can trust me. I am the kind of person who says what I mean. I will deliver what I promise."

Trust has become a devalued word. It's not that the people asking others to trust them are dishonest. It's that trust, even when received, is qualified. We know of two real estate organizations that partnered on a development deal. They promised to split research costs equally, but it turned out that one put in much more time doing surveys and investigating environmental impact issues than the other. So the one that invested more time felt that its alliance partner should pay more. The partner countered that this was unfair because it had put in more time searching for outside funding for the venture.

The lesson is that alliance partners must think about their commitments before they make them and stick to them once made. Trust is hard-won and easily shattered. The damage done by going back on a previously agreed-upon provision is incalculable. Power of Two alliances don't do this sort of thing.

Instead they work at building trust with unusual single-mindedness and seriousness of purpose. Specifically, Power of Two allies build trust seven ways. They do the following:

- Discuss it up front
- Make the first move
- Bring a business opportunity
- Reveal intentions
- Set realistic expectations
- Eliminate hidden agendas
- Treat one another as equals

Discuss It Up Front

"Can I trust you?" is not the way to begin this discussion. Instead, communicate how important trust is to you and how it acts as the basis for a Power of Two alliance. Once consensus is achieved on this general point, talk about specifics. One of the best ways we've found to do this is by generating "what ifs":

What if a prospective alliance customer says it wants to work with you but not me? How do we respond?

What if one of us feels we're putting in more time, money, or effort than the other? How do we deal with it?

What if we can't communicate on an issue or reach consensus? What if one of us decides to take matters into our own hands and act independently to achieve an alliance goal? Is this acceptable alliance behavior?

What if an opportunity presents itself that requires changing the alliance agreement, structure, goals, or the like? How can we make changes without either of us feeling that we've betrayed the original purpose of the alliance?

Too often organizations deal with trust as a matter of instinct. A champion "just knows" he can trust his counterpart. One person has worked with another for years and "trusts him like I would trust my brother." Certainly instinct plays a role. But many complex issues are involved in an alliance that instinct can't anticipate. Only when these issues are articulated and kicked around do both parties really set the stage for a trusting relationship.

We have a small business client that spent years forming alliances based on his intuition. He claimed he could sense who was trustworthy; he said that if someone didn't look him in the eye or had a weak handshake or hemmed and hawed when asked a tough question, his instincts would kick in and he'd know they weren't the right organization to partner with. When he contacted us, however, he had begun to question his instincts. In recent years he had

endured three alliance partnerships that failed because of trust issues—it turned out that one of his alliance partners was a brilliant
liar and was later indicted for fraud.

This client now uses a number of "what-ifs" at the start of every
relationship, exploring scenarios with alliance partners to determine if they share the same ideas about trust. Though this up-front
discussion doesn't guarantee a trusting relationship, it's a better
method than relying on unsubstantiated hunches and instincts.

Make the First Move

In *The 7 Habits of Highly Effective People* (Simon & Schuster, 1990),
Stephen Covey points out that building trust involves making small
commitments and then keeping them. This process builds what he
calls the "emotional bank account" of trust. Power of Two allies can
develop trust by following a similar approach. Champions can do
little things in the beginning of their relationship to establish trust,
such as returning phone calls promptly, not canceling meetings at
the drop of a hat, keeping deadlines, and coming prepared to meetings. They gain confidence in each other through personal interac-
tion with each other and their organizations. So many times we
have seen these things not happen. Excuses are made: "I had a commitment with a customer, but the legal guys didn't get the contract
finished." Champions can't deal with each other on this level. They
are the keepers of the trust.

At times one alliance partner won't be able to keep a commitment because of something beyond its control. If it has developed a
reputation for meeting commitments, then the champions will be
able to repair the damage to the relationship. If not, the champion
will have a difficult time convincing his organization that next time
the other company will come through.

Say or do something that makes you slightly vulnerable. Show
your partner that you're willing to take a risk as a way of communicating your trust. Don't demand reciprocity—"You tell me a secret
and I'll tell you one." Start the ball rolling and see how your al-

liance partner reacts. The things you can do run the gamut, including the following:

- Reveal sensitive information.
- Tell your partner about a weakness of your organization.
- Recount a failure or mistake your partner might not know about.

Then observe your partner's reaction. Do you receive sensitive information or stories of weakness or failure in return? Or is your vulnerability used against you? Does the partner spread word within the alliance or outside it about your vulnerable area? Does it become an issue in future discussions that turns into an obstacle?

How an ally responds to this first trusting move on your part gives you a good indication how it will respond in the future. If it responds well, it gives you a base to build on and makes you more willing to reveal vulnerable aspects of your organization to your ally.

Bring a Business Opportunity

This is the trust litmus test. Simply bringing an opportunity to the table—even if it doesn't result in anything—draws alliance partners closer together. It's an act of good faith, demonstrating that you believe enough in the alliance to bring in a prospect. Until then everything is just talk, but this is a meaningful action. Consider this case:

> Several years ago we were involved in alliance discussions between two competitors in the European market. They had not had any positive interaction at all. Many times they approached the same customers and worked at cross purposes, sometimes even to the detriment of the customer. An alliance champion from one organization came from the United States to see what he could do; there seemed to be hope, as the two organizations had found a way to work successfully together in America. But he found a lot of bad blood and no trust at all between the two.

Still, a few individuals in his organization knew an executive in the other organization. They had met and talked at an industry conference. In planning for a joint executive meeting the next day, he encountered one individual who insisted that the whole organization was dishonest. Well, it's pretty hard to find an outfit where everyone is a liar, and this wasn't one; the champion knew that because he'd worked with the company back in the States. In a private discussion, he asked the executive from his company who was going to lead the meeting to come with an open mind—to think of a customer that could really use the competitor's help, perhaps, or even to pretend for a moment that the two companies weren't competitors.

The next day, discussion between the two companies was cordial. There was talk of trying to work together, but the champion didn't see how it would lead anywhere. Then the lead executive did something that shocked the other executives on his team and the competitor sitting across the table. He told them about an opportunity of which they had no knowledge. He said, "Let's work on this one together. You be the prime contractor. We will work for you on this business proposal." The mood in the room changed. The discussion focused on the business. A point of contact was established for each company. The alliance went on to win the business because no one else in the market could match its combined capabilities. The two companies teamed on many other opportunities after that. They continued to be competitors, but trust had been established.

Just as important, bringing in a business opportunity presents another type of opportunity: to surface and resolve trust-related issues. We know of a recently formed alliance that had a chance to set up an office in a new market. Though the members ultimately decided against it, they had to make some tough decisions together. Just going through the process increased their mutual respect and trust.

When you bring a business opportunity to an alliance, here are some do's and don'ts related to trust building.

Do:

- Treat your partner's ideas and suggestions with respect; encourage its representatives to offer their opinion about the opportunity, even if you're the one that brought it to the table.

- Be honest about what you think of the opportunity; express your reservations about the alliance's ability to capitalize on it as well as your reasons for pursuing it further.

- Project where the opportunity may take the alliance; talk about the requirements of pursuing the opportunity (time, money, creativity, and the like) and what each partner must contribute to pursue it successfully; look into the future so that you can identify concerns, fears, and doubts about working with your partner on this project.

Don't:

- Shy away from sensitive areas related to the opportunity; don't miss the chance to determine how you both handle touchy issues and if you're willing to be honest and open; don't avoid conflict or confrontation.

- Lord the opportunity over your alliance partner; don't use it to put yourself in a one-up position simply because you brought it to the alliance's attention; don't lose your partner's trust by upsetting the delicate balance of power.

- Use your partner only as a resource to capitalize on the opportunity; don't take all the brainstorming and strategizing responsibilities for yourself and leave the dirty work for your ally; don't act as if you're the brains of the alliance and it's the brawn.

As you work together and meet with people outside the alliance in order to explore an opportunity, think about the following questions:

Do you find that you and your ally are exchanging ideas, information, and other resources freely?

Do any minor irritations or problems give you pause? Can you identify a specific incident that makes you feel that your partner isn't being completely open and honest?

Do any major irritations or problems give you pause? Can you identify a specific incident that makes you feel that your partner is being deceptive or dishonest?

During your pursuit of the opportunity, does your alliance partner do anything that strikes you as especially generous and or that demonstrates its trust in you? Do you demonstrate the same trusting behavior in working with them?

Reveal Intentions

Power of Two alliances form within a larger alliance infrastructure network. As a result, you may form different alliances with different organizations at different times. It's fine to partner with one organization for one opportunity and another for the next, but you need to be clear about your intentions. Nothing creates distrust faster than when a prospective partner feels you've misled it about working together on an opportunity, or when an organization thinks you've united to go after an opportunity but you back out at the last second.

To make your intentions known, do the following:

Tell your alliance partner you won't pursue a specific type of opportunity with any other company. In other words, let it know that the two of you will partner exclusively in a specific market, product, or other category. Power of Two allies take much of the uncertainty and doubt out of the relationship by pledging to work together for a common goal no matter what. We've seen many other collaborative efforts where an unwillingness to make this pledge created great distrust. Here's one:

A small design firm and a mid-sized automobile parts manufacturing company decided to partner on opportunities in what they felt would be an exploding (pardon the pun) air bag market. They had exchanged a great deal of information and ideas, though they hadn't yet begun working on specific projects together. During this time, the manufacturing company was contacted by a larger design firm that had done a great deal of work for General Motors. The manufacturer told the smaller design firm that it still wanted to work together, but also wanted to be free to pursue air bag system opportunities with the other design firm. As you might suspect, the small design company felt betrayed and vowed never to work with the manufacturer on any project again.

If you haven't decided on an alliance partner for a specific type of opportunity, let everyone in your alliance network know that you're playing the field. Power of Two alliances are difficult to form if you're viewed as secretive or even deceptive in seeking an ally. Communicate to all potential alliance partners that you're searching for a company to collaborate with for a specific purpose. Don't tell three companies and fail to inform four others. Being egalitarian in this matter has a Power of Two benefit—it allows you the maximum flexibility in partnering. When everyone in your network knows you're looking at Opportunity X and want to form an alliance to go after it, you've given all your potential allies the chance to step forward with ideas and resources. You've also decreased the chances that a future ally will feel left out.

Make a quick decision. Don't string along all the companies in your network. Making quick decisions about who you want to partner with will help avoid lost opportunities for others. A large, well-known corporation in the consumer electronics industry interviewed scores of smaller consulting firms for a possible alliance partnership. Needless to say, all the consulting firms were excited about the opportunity. The interviewing process, however, dragged on for fifteen months! When the corporation made its decision, it left many angry consulting firms in its wake because they had had to sit on the sidelines for many months instead of taking action on their own or with another partner. If you're playing the field, fine, but play it fast.

Make a commitment and stick to it. Sometimes alliances begin with the best of intentions but one partner gets cold feet along the way. Power of Two alliances demand consistency from both parties. Doubts, concerns, and questions about an opportunity should be aired before the Power of Two alliance forms, not after. Traditional alliances are notorious for broken commitments—just look at all the deal makers that have been sued by their alliance partners for failing to live up to their commitments. Power of Two allies may change direction, alter strategy, and increase or decrease the speed with which they seek an opportunity. But once they make a commitment to pursue it, they don't back out on their alliance partners. Consider this case:

One start-up company with great technology was growing like gang-busters but knew it needed alliance partners to continue to grow and to survive in the long run. It hired an executive to head up the alliance strategy. He was overwhelmed immediately. Even though he hired some people to help him, he had to be in the middle of every deal; he was really a deal maker and got his thrills from it. He positioned himself as the champion who knew the strategy of his organization and had the ear of the top executives in the company. So the alliance champions took his word when he said he would do something—for about four months. He made so many commitments to so many people that he lost track. Based on the resources his company had, in fact, he overcommitted. The other alliance champions began to seek other avenues of communication into the company, and finally for other companies to ally with.

Business practices are just as important as products and services. This little company is going to stay little if it doesn't find a new alliance champion. He will never be trusted by some of the champions he left standing empty-handed when it counted.

Set Realistic Expectations

Or to put it another way: don't oversell your ally on the rewards or undersell them on the risks. This is a common practice in traditional alliance partnerships. To convince a company that it should collaborate, some organizations wax rhapsodic about the profit potential and minimize the risk of losing money. In the old paradigm this was expected behavior to a certain extent; you went into a deal figuring your alliance partner was being "creative" with its risk-to-reward scenario. Power of Two allies, however, try to set realistic expectations. They allow the opportunity to dictate expectations rather than wishful thinking or the desire to rope in a partner.

Still, even Power of Two alliances sometimes find that expectations become distorted. The cause may be a misinterpreted remark, the excitement of the moment, or a million other things. As a result, one ally is angry at the other because things aren't happening as quickly as expected, or because it thinks the other failed to mention an important piece of information to draw it into a project.

When misperceived expectations breed distrust, champions are invaluable. Management teams in Power of Two alliances step back and have champions reset alliance expectations, allowing them to use their strong relationships to get everyone back on the same page. Champions are terrific at calming people down, communicating facts, and dispelling fictions. Because they have established a strong bond with their fellow champions, they are in a good position to figure out what went wrong and how it can be put right.

Eliminate Hidden Agendas

In many alliances organizations almost feel entitled to hidden agendas, viewing them as harmless. But they do cause harm. They communicate to an alliance partner that you were not completely honest and up front about why you wanted to collaborate. Even with a hidden agenda you still may achieve your alliance goals, but you taint the alliance and make it difficult if not impossible to maintain a high level of trust.

Hidden agendas come in all shapes and sizes, and we don't have the space to list all of the ones we've witnessed. Here are just a few:

- To form relationships with the alliance partner's network
- To use the alliance to achieve one goal and then proceed independently or with another alliance partner toward more ambitious goals
- To gain access to an alliance partner's proprietary technology
- To capitalize on the experience of working with a "name" partner (to be able to tell future partners that "we worked with this Fortune 200 company on that project")
- To use the alliance partnership as a recruiting tool (hiring away a partner's key people)

Some of these agendas would be acceptable in Power of Two alliances if they weren't hidden. If you incorporate learning about a given technology into the alliance agreement, for instance, it ceases to be a problem. Many companies, however, are not accustomed to being open and honest about all their goals. They keep them squirreled away, as if a deal isn't worthwhile unless one has secret goals as well as stated ones.

Sometimes hidden agendas develop after the fact—after the alliance is up and running. Say, for example, that during the course of an alliance partnership with Ally ABC, Ally XYZ comes up with a great new service concept. Though XYZ develops this concept in part because of information gleaned from ABC, it doesn't feel compelled to share the concept with its alliance partner. But it still intends to work with ABC to achieve the alliance's objectives, which can be done without discussing the service innovation. When XYZ formerly launches its new service a year later, however, ABC feels as if XYZ was not aboveboard in its dealings. Though XYZ didn't violate the letter of the alliance agreement, it violated the spirit.

Which brings up a related point: don't expect to hide your agenda from an alliance partner indefinitely. Sometimes organizations feel that what an alliance partner doesn't know about won't hurt it. The flaw in that reasoning is that it's difficult to keep things hidden from a company you're working with. For one thing, secrecy breeds leaks—there's nothing like a hidden agenda to get people talking. For another thing, some people in an organization will feel bad about their hidden agendas and inform their partners about what's going on.

In Power of Two alliances there are no private goals, only alliance goals.

Treat One Another as Equals

Trust is tough to come by in relationships where one alliance partner holds the balance of power and acts like it. Power of Two alliances, by definition, involve dissimilar organizations: big and small, supplier and customer, Industry A and Industry B, market leaders and market followers. Power of Two allies are usually similar internally (they have shared values) but often quite different externally.

For Power of Two alliances to work, there needs to be a level playing field. If one partner feels dominated or intimidated it will never be willing to offer all the ideas and resources it's capable of offering. It'll become overreliant on the bigger partner; it'll be reluctant to express some of its more creative or risky ideas, believing their partner will find them foolish.

Without equality between allies, the synergy that exists in Power of Two alliances will be absent—there won't be an equal and free-flowing exchange of information, products, services, concepts, and so on. More importantly, distrust will surface at the slightest miscommunication or misinterpretation.

"Perhaps we should shift our focus to a new market segment in light of the poor sales for our product," Champion A said to Champion B. B could easily have taken this as an accusation, for B's company was responsible for the sales effort that had gone poorly. B, however, did not view A's statement as unfair or uncalled for. Sales were poor, and looking at a new segment was a logical strategy. Their equal footing ensured that they could talk about this sensitive issue without breaking their bond of trust.

Power of Two allies frequently challenge each other without throwing down their gloves and dueling. They are willing to say things like: "You have the best research facility in the country; why aren't we using it to explore markets in Third World countries?" In ordinary partnerships, both companies can be overly cautious and reserved in their dealings with each other. Because they fear to offend, they also fail to push each other to outstanding performance. Equality gives allies the courage to so push.

It also produces creative tension. Power of Two alliances crackle with tension; ideas fly like sparks when the two champions get together. The trust level is so high that champions don't hold back ideas; they feel comfortable enough that they can let loose with even the most out-of-the-box thoughts. We've been in meetings between allies where you can see the energy in the animated faces and hear it in the passion of their voices. Each partner trusts the other not to make fun of their ideas or put them down. They aren't shy about exploring both worst- and best-case scenarios. But this creative tension is missing from many traditional partnerships:

A graphics packaging company we worked with partnered with a Fortune 500 corporation that wanted to make use of the packaging company's binding services. Though the packaging company was able to expand its staff and make a nice short-term profit because of this partnership, it never achieved any larger goals. Terms of the partnership were dictated by the corporation. The smaller company never completely trusted its larger partner; it was always reluctant to volunteer its best ideas for fear that the bigger company would usurp them. Ultimately, the partnership dissolved because the packaging firm felt more like a supplier than a partner. The financial gain didn't make up for the lack of independence and initiative. To this day the packaging firm is convinced that the partnership could have been much more profitable for both companies had it been allowed to contribute more than services to the partnership.

Trust Analysis Questions

Though it's difficult to know in advance if a prospective partner is willing and able to build a high-trust partnership, you may want to pose the following questions to get a reading of the partner's ideas on this front. We want to emphasize that there are no right answers to these, just answers you feel comfortable with. Answer them yourself first, then see how your prospective partner's answers jibe.

- Would any events or situations cause you to pull out of the alliance after making a commitment to it? Which ones? Would there be any way to adjust and keep the original partnership commitment?

- Would you be willing to share any information requested, no questions asked? What information would you be unwilling to share and why?

- Is someone in your organization trusted implicitly by everyone who would make a good champion? Give an example or tell a story that illustrates why this person is so trustworthy.

- In past collaborations and alliances, have you been completely open and honest with your partners? If not, what prevented you or them from being open and honest?

- If a bigger company with more resources were to approach you about forming an alliance, would you agree even though you had made a commitment to partner with us? Would you expect us to turn down a similar offer?

Chapter Ten

Cultural Criteria

Power of Two partners don't need to possess mirror-image cultures. They do have to possess an understanding of each other's culture and the communication capabilities to overcome whatever cultural conflicts arise during the course of the alliance.

The purpose of this chapter is not to make judgments about which cultures are good or bad for alliances. It is simply to alert you to the fact that speed and flexibility aren't possible without some degree of cross-cultural understanding. Too often we've seen alliance partnerships founder because one company's way of doing things couldn't be reconciled with another company's modus operandi. Even when both partners' champions and management were committed to the alliance, their efforts slowed to a crawl or they were unable to change directions because of cultural issues—or, more precisely, because they failed to address the key cultural differences that ultimately sabotage alliances.

Think about a few common cultural variations:

- One company takes forever to make decisions or react to problems because of an entrenched chain of command; another is far more entrepreneurial and empowers people to decide with minimal or no approvals.

- One organization has an open culture and shares information freely; another is more cautious and has strict policies and procedures about information exchanges.

- One corporation has strong traditions of training its people and promoting from within; another routinely searches outside for the people it needs.

What would happen if you were to partner with an organization with a different culture? How would your company react when your counterpart takes forever to supply you with key data? How would you feel if you went forward on a project together and your company felt you could train the project people to get the job done but your alliance partner insists that people with the requisite skills be hired?

Power of Two alliances address potential cultural conflicts by examining the following issues:

1. Who are the key influencers who get things done?
2. How do things get accomplished?
3. How are the people motivated and measured?
4. What is the intracompany communications flow?
5. How does the company communicate with other organizations?
6. What is the philosophy of the company on customer service?

Who Are the Key Influencers?

One mistake many alliances make that denies them Power of Two status is assuming that one or two key people can make or break the alliance. An organization figures that if it gets buy-in from its partner's relationship manager, that's good enough. Or a small group from Company A meets with a small group from Company B, and they get on famously; they conclude that because they can work together well, the alliance will function smoothly.

In reality alliances bring a wide variety of people into the picture—people besides those who arranged for the alliance. Every culture has many different influencers who can facilitate or obstruct the alliance as it pursues opportunities. Power of Two alliances are well aware of the influencers in both cultures, and they work hard to enlist the aid of the positive influencers to combat the effects of the negative influencers.

You can do this by listing all the people you know at your organization who may have some influence on your alliance strategy; they're the people who control resources or possess skills the alliance will need or who have the political or decision-making power that will impact alliance requirements. Look at the executive team, division heads, sales management, product development, marketing, customer service, purchasing, and the like. Then rate them using the following categories:

1. *Alliance-phobic*. These people feel alliances are a waste of time; they may even believe that they're a counterproductive business strategy. Alliance-phobics may just not be capable of any type of collaboration; they probably don't do well working on internal teams. Don't assign these people alliance-related responsibilities. Make sure your alliance partner takes the same precautions.

2. *Disinterested*. These individuals don't think much of alliances, but they're not hostile toward them. It's difficult to get them energized and actively working for alliance goals. They can even provide de facto barriers to alliance goals because of their apathy; they may veto additional expenditures that the alliance requires because it just doesn't seem that important to them. They can harm the alliance, but they're not looking to do so.

3. *Fence-straddlers*. You have to be careful with people in this group; they can help you or hurt you. They won't necessarily turn around and support the alliance initiative like a champion would, but they also won't stand in the way. They're often swayed by the opinions of others. If the majority view is that alliances are good, they'll often vote with the majority and can be counted on to further alliance aims. If there's no

clear consensus about partnering, however, you might exercise some caution in assigning these people important alliance responsibilities.

4. *Supporters.* They're team players and collaborators within the organization; they've either participated in alliances before or are well versed in what they're all about. They applaud the company's alliance making and recognize it as part of the new business paradigm. They are good influencers. They just need a champion to get behind, and they will move an alliance opportunity forward.

5. *Proactive.* People in this group are powerfully influential. They serve as assistant champions. Not only do they recognize that the future of their organization rests on its ability to make Power of Two alliances but they want to contribute to the success of these alliances. They search out alliance opportunities and look for an internal champion to spearhead the initiative.

To a certain extent you can't do much about those with 1 or 2 ratings. In many cases all you can do is identify people who might throw up barriers and be aware of their obstructionist tendencies. More importantly, nurture relationships with influencers who have 3, 4, and especially 5 ratings. They're the ones who will help you solve the problems that arise as your two organizations begin working together. When your cultures clash, they'll come up with ideas, provide resources, and do whatever is necessary to keep the alliance intact and moving forward.

It's important to be aware of the influencers within your partner's organization, not just your own. You may need the help of your partner's champion to accomplish this task, but it's well worth it. We've found that establishing a circle of influence within a partner's organization can greatly accelerate decision making, especially when your partner is a large organization. Don't let the size of a company influence you. You may assume large companies will take a long time to get things done, but that's not always true, and we can prove it:

We once worked with a service company that wanted to move forward on an initiative with a very large manufacturing company with a very large sales organization. We began nurturing a relationship with a middle-level executive in a key business unit, and he eventually became our champion within the manufacturing company. He had developed a network of relationships in his current business unit and in others he had worked in over the years. Leveraging these relationships, he took our alliance proposal to the business unit executive team and obtained its agreement to move forward. With the management team's approval, our new-found champion was able to secure the resources and support of his peers inside and outside the business unit. It took days to do this, not weeks. Because our champion knew the key influencers and decision makers, he overcame what appeared to us outsiders a formidable obstacle: getting approval for an alliance initiative that had never been done before by this manufacturing company. It would have been a long, drawn-out process if we had followed standard channels of communication and approval.

Large company cultures generally force their smaller partners to navigate through a nightmarish approval process. If you're partnering with a big company, you should capitalize on influencers you've rated 3 through 5 to circumvent that process.

How Do Things Get Accomplished?

People sometimes complain that alliances are a lot of talk but no action. In fact, we've heard more than one relationship manager lambaste his organization because "it's impossible to figure out how things really get done around here." Power of Two allies make sure they know both the informal and formal protocols. Though the procedural manual may detail the precise method for gaining budgeting for a project, savvy managers understand the informal shortcuts that can save time and save the alliance the money it needs.

It's great to discuss with your counterpart how you'll go about getting approvals, who needs to sign off before implementation can begin, and so on, but it's probably more valuable to ask your partner about the unofficial ways things get done. To find out, ask the following questions:

When you need more money than has been budgeted, what's the easiest and fastest way to get it?

When momentum on a project stalls because consensus can't be achieved, what people are skilled at breaking the deadlock and getting the project moving again?

If you need to pull people off their regular jobs for a special assignment, who can best help you do it? The person's immediate supervisor? Someone higher up in the corporate ranks?

When a division head or some other top manager refuses to provide the resources you need, what's the best way to get around that person and secure those resources?

How do people in your company convince the decision makers to take a significant risk? Does management respond best to formal, detailed presentations or informal one-one-one discussions?

Funding issues often drive alliance partners crazy. We can't count the number of times we've heard a relationship manager complain that "our partner told us she's only empowered to spend $50,000 on new business opportunities, and she doesn't think she can get approval for the additional $50,000 we need"—or something similar. What happens next? Should the alliance ask a regional manager or a vice president of sales to make a decision? Does the marketing or product management team have to be involved? Is there a special reserve fund that the money can come out of? Can the alliance form a subsidiary and obtain a loan from an outside financial institution?

Anticipating and preparing for roadblocks and stalemates is what Power of Two allies routinely do. They assume that at some point they're going to have to be creative in order to accomplish the alliance's strategy. When the process threatens to grind to a halt, they need to know how to work each organization's subculture.

How Are People Motivated and Measured?

Perhaps a better question is: Does each organization reward team as well as individual performance? If the answer is yes, the odds are that their cultures will give people incentive to achieve alliance goals. Unfortunately, many organizations still have cultures that prize the individual over the group; they have a history of rewarding individual initiative and performance, and their formal and informal incentives confirm it. For example, does your alliance partner have a sales force whose members are only compensated when they personally sell a product or service? In other words, if you and your partner jointly sell a product or service, will the sales force be rewarded? If not, they will view the alliance as competition and do nothing to help further alliance goals.

To avoid this problem, compensation could be redesigned so that your partner's sales reps share a percentage of each sale made by the alliance. Many companies have agreements that provide compensation for sales people that run from 80 to 125 percent of their normal compensation when an alliance partner sells a solution that includes their joint products and services. This arrangement provides an incentive for the sales people to support the efforts of the alliance. These companies have set up their measurement and compensation plans as "channel neutral," which means that whoever sells the products creates a realized sale for the sales force.

Certainly sales force motivation is a key issue when alliances are created. Just as important, however, is the motivation and measurement of other groups who will provide resources and services to the alliance. Power of Two alliances are careful not to overlook other critical functions, teams, and individuals. Too often partners fail to assess what cultural norms need adjusting when companies join forces. In one culture, technological innovation is esteemed. In another, marketing brilliance is prized. Compensation systems reflect these norms. But when an alliance is created the norms can be in conflict, or there may be confusion and misunderstanding about exactly what and who will be rewarded if the alliance succeeds.

So make sure you establish and communicate the skills that the alliance values and the rewards and recognition that await those who contribute these skills. This recognition is significant. A critical task is to help people understand that the alliance needs and will recognize their contributions. It's easy for people to jump to conclusions and assume that an alliance culture doesn't value what they do, that it's only designed for one group or to achieve a narrow goal. Sometimes all it takes is a relationship manager or champion communicating what people's roles are within the alliance framework and how alliance tasks relate to their jobs and careers. When people understand something as basic as this, they often change from being disinterested in the alliance to being strong supporters.

What Is the Intracompany Communications Flow?

Many companies have cultures where communication is ad hoc and selective. People don't always know everything they need to know when they need to know it; sometimes they're cut out of the main communication loop and sometimes they have to learn things in a roundabout fashion. This may not be a big problem when the company is operating independently, but it's a major issue in an alliance.

Power of Two alliances need to move fast, to change direction on a dime. They can't do that if the internal lines of communication are poor. Here are three things you can do if you're burdened with an uncommunicative culture:

Use informal and formal meetings to discuss alliance-related topics. Yes, most people hate meetings. Still, they are a necessary evil and preferable to the alternative—a lack of group, face-to-face discussions. Power of Two companies use meetings to create alliance cultures where ideas and knowledge are exchanged freely. For example, Steelcase uses informal groups they call innovation teams that meet every Friday. These meetings have some structure, but they're also very flexible and encourage people to take risks with their idea sharing. When you can turn alliance meetings into fun, creative forums (instead of boring lectures where one person dominates the discussion), then they'll help create an alliance culture within the organization.

Produce newsletters that entertain, provoke, and inform. Newsletters, like meetings, tend to be dull. They don't have to be. We've seen alliances create terrific newsletters that don't operate under the same restrictions and follow the same vanilla formats as most corporate newsletters. There's the chance to be more creative, to tackle taboo subjects, to explore the nature of alliances. Sometimes existing corporate newsletters can include an alliance section that's equally innovative. Don't use newsletters simply as a tool to list dates and events. Though it can work as an information source, it also needs to stimulate thought and action.

Capitalize on technology to exchange alliance knowledge faster and better. Many companies are using e-mail, internal web pages, or both to communicate with their employees. Take advantage of on-line newsletters. A number of organizations have built extensive electronic networks where most knowledge is transferred through internal office memos and news group exchanges; they're also getting involved with on-line conferences that offer chats among team members in different facilities. You can create electronic distribution lists and special interest groups to get critical information about the alliance out to those who need to know. This medium also enables you to create news broadcasts and success stories in real time so people don't have to hear about what the alliance is doing secondhand; it also reduces the rumor-mongering that plagues many partnerships.

Not all internal communications are valuable; they may even be a drain on the budget. Here's an example:

> We worked with a company that published a quarterly newsletter for
> each of its top ten alliances. The intent was to gain visibility for the

alliance organization within the company. The initial newsletters included photos of and interviews with vice presidents extolling the value of the relationship and the alliance organization. Each quarter the relationship manager for each alliance searched for ideas and success stories to grab the attention of the internal audience. They also used the newsletters to demonstrate their alliance commitment to their partners. They sent hundreds of copies of the newsletter to key people in their partners' organizations as well as their own. This strategy continued for two years, but the relationship managers didn't get many calls from their audience seeking additional information on business opportunities or offering new ones. No new business opportunities could be attributed to the newsletter; eventually the expense of producing it became a budget issue and it died a quiet death. None of the relationship managers ever received a call asking what happened to the newsletter, confirming that very few had ever really read it or found it useful. The relationship managers had complained almost from the beginning about the amount of their time it took to get the newsletter published and distributed while the information in it was still relevant.

Our recommendation is that you imbed your alliance information into existing company newsletters that have gained reader loyalty. This tactic will help leverage your credibility as a viable strategic growth initiative. Slowly, you can get influencers in the organization to endorse your efforts. Over time you will become accepted readily as a necessary part of your organization's success.

How Does a Company Communicate Outside?

In other words, how will you communicate with your alliance partner and the outside world? Some cultures are tight-lipped and rarely release important information to the media. Others are very open and constantly communicate with trade publications. We've seen collaborations where alliance partners routinely "forgot" to inform each other about key initiatives or miscommunicated their intent;

they were simply following their culture's dictate that the more your name is in the press the better.

From the very start, Power of Two allies agree on what will be communicated to whom and when. This begins with a public relations strategy (especially if it's a high-profile alliance). We've worked with companies that aggressively leveraged the names of their alliance partners in press releases. That's fine as long as both alliance partners agree. Some of the public relations issues that should be discussed include these:

- How to refer to the alliance when dealing with the media (in terms of alliance goals, tactics, name of alliance, duration, and similar matters)
- When and how to announce the alliance formation; when and how to announce achieving an alliance goal
- Whether a brochure or other materials should be produced and included in an alliance press kit
- Who should be the media spokesperson for the alliance
- What issues are off-limits to the media
- What nonmedia collaborations are acceptable (speaking engagements, trade show appearances, and the like)

Power of Two allies don't use each other—that is, take advantage of each other without consent. In the old partnership paradigm companies used each other all the time. It was not uncommon to find an organization partnering with the covert purpose of exploiting the name value of a bigger partner.

This is unacceptable behavior in a Power of Two alliance. Unless the ground rules are set in advance, however, one of the partners may be tempted to take advantage in this or a similar way:

We once worked with a small, private company that had developed an excellent product. Because it didn't have the resources to bring its product to market on its own, it partnered with a much larger

organization. They had signed a formal alliance agreement to introduce the new product and were pursuing a number of different opportunities together when the larger corporation learned that the
smaller was planning a public stock offering in the next quarter. As
part of that offering the small company had prepared a prospectus
that emphasized the alliance with the large corporation; it also in-
tended to stress the partnership in a press release due to be sent to financial reporters. The corporation felt manipulated. Though the
partner had never lied, it had also not been completely honest about
its ulterior motive for the alliance. Ultimately this manipulation created distrust and eventually resulted in the end of the alliance.

Answering the following questions will establish some interalliance communication ground rules:

What is the review process for interalliance or outside
   communications?

Who will do the reviewing?

When will the review be done?

How will you communicate to develop a specific business
   opportunity?

Most alliances we are involved with entail alliance champions
reviewing initiatives monthly or quarterly while the executives review them annually. The review can be in person or through documentation that addresses the original parameters of success. Either
way, the review process is absolutely critical to maintaining a good
communications flow. The review should respond to such questions
as these:

What goals were we to have achieved at this point?

How close are we to our projected goals?

What do we need to do to better meet our goals between now
   and the next review?

What did we do well that we can leverage during this next period between reviews?

Who has shown exceptional performance during this time?

What methodology of communications works well?

Who has communicated well with others?

What can we learn from these people?

What new methods should we try to improve communications?

The point of all this isn't just to facilitate a good flow of ideas and information. The objective is to establish an alliance culture that eliminates hidden agendas and minimizes covert actions. Power of Two allies are terrific at talking about uncomfortable issues in advance; they establish protocols for communicating when things go wrong or when a problem crops us. Here are some issues that should be addressed up front:

- How to communicate with existing customers of each partner; what customers should be approached and how the alliance should be positioned to them; what customers cannot be approached by the alliance
- How to communicate failures; the importance of delivering bad news to each other quickly and without sugar-coating; the importance of not blaming each other when discussing failure
- How to communicate about conflicts and personality clashes; the need to avoid assessing personal blame and deal only with the issues

What Is the Potential Partner's Customer Philosophy?

Collaborative efforts often result in a mutual customer. As you're probably aware, there are a wide variety of cultural biases toward customers. If those biases aren't exposed and discussed—and if consensus isn't achieved early on about how to deal with that mu-tual customer—the alliance won't last. Consider this case:

> Two automobile after-market product companies partnered to es-tablish a strong European presence with a new product they in-tended to develop together. One company took a very aggressive approach to its customers; it constantly challenged them and at-tempted to secure more business from them. The other company had a much more laid-back approach; its was a gentlemanly, reactive stance. As astonishing as it might seem, these two companies didn't talk to each other about their style of dealing with customers. They had only discussed who each other's customers were and the cus-tomer segment in Europe that should be targeted.
>
> As a result, all hell broke loose when they started to sell the new product. On more than one occasion the alliance sales team almost came to blows after prospective customer meetings. It's possible that their customer approaches were so diametrically opposed that they never should have partnered in the first place. It's more likely, how-ever, that they could have arrived at some middle ground if they had simply aired their customer philosophies.

What's your customer philosophy, and how does it compare to your ally's? The following questions will serve as focal points for making that determination:

Is there a greater focus on product or service quality?

Is there a significant amount of open communication with the customer? Are lines of communication restricted in any way?

What degree of cynicism exists in attitudes toward customers?

How is the customer service staff recognized and compen-sated? How is it motivated (employee of the month con-tests, other ways)?

Does the culture empower customer service people to make decisions related to the customer or do they have to pass those decisions on to management?

What are the policies regarding customer complaints or dissat-
isfaction with products or services? Are there warranty
issues?

What sort of process is in place to handle customer orders—
fulfillment systems, shipping procedures, computer systems?

How do you deal with missed deadlines and communicating
other problems to customers?

Is yours a culture of people working overtime to solve customer problems (or of passing the buck and looking for
excuses)?

How is the customer service staff recognized and compen-
sated? Are there programs in place to enhance productivity
and performance? Is the environment one of motivation by
fear or empowerment?

Do employees pass a problem along to someone else or do they
take ownership of a customer concern until it is resolved?

It's likely that you and any partner will answer these questions
differently. That's fine, and the point of this exercise isn't to judge
your ally's customer philosophy. What you want to avoid, however,
is reacting rather than responding to your partner's philosophy.
That is, don't put yourself in the position of reacting negatively
when you see how your collaborator deals with customers. Respond
positively to the gaps, to what you feel is missing. For instance, if
your partner routinely takes forty-eight hours to fill customer orders
and you believe it should take only twenty-four, the two of you need
to talk about how the alliance can use your methodology to achieve
that. Ideally the alliance customer philosophy will represent the
best of both worlds. Here's an example:

One company we worked with, a large manufacturer, surveyed its
business partners and customers twice a year. It used a third party
company to do this to ensure that it was done on time and that the
results were communicated as given by the customer or business
partner. The survey was simple and short.

Lots of companies do surveys. Many feel it's a waste of time. But this company was different, because each negative response from a customer was escalated to the responsible business unit executive. The executive then asked for a plan to fix the problem and got back to the customer with it. With this attitude and response, the customers and business partners of this manufacturing company were happy to spend time giving feedback on the shortcomings of the business relationship.

If you find that your potential alliance partner's customer service philosophy is not in alignment with yours, be very cautious. In our customer-driven society the customer will continually demand better and better service. If your potential alliance partner does not have a service mentality, it may be too costly to try to provide one given the need for speed and response to your customers' needs.

Chapter Eleven

The Future of Alliances

There is no "us" and "them" anymore. The us-against-the-world posture of ruggedly individualistic corporations is ill-suited to a global marketplace. Today, and especially in the future, the enemy is not competitors or industry regulators or the economy. The enemy is our inability to see all the different ways we can partner with others to capitalize on rapidly multiplying opportunities.

Not everyone sees it this way. The organizational landscape is still filled with reactionaries—companies that react to market conditions by attempting to "beat" their competitors. There's still a bunker mentality, a sense that when things get tough the organization has to become more insular and draw on its own resources to outthink, outwork, and outinnovate the competition.

Unfortunately, our resources are too limited. Companies have outsourced many of their precious resources; they've downsized a lot of talent; they've sold off divisions with precious assets that were hurting their quarterly performance. These trends are going to continue. Until organizations recognize their own mortality—that at some point in the future their diminishing resources will no longer sustain them—they'll continue to ignore what's becoming obvious to everyone else: alliances are the future.

And not just any type of alliance. The Power of Two alliance dovetails with a number of current, emerging, and predicted trends. Let's examine these trends and see how they increase the attractiveness of the Power of Two concept.

Trend No. 1

Leaner Big Companies, Fatter and More Plentiful Little Ones

People will continue leaving big companies in droves. Not only will they be downsized and divested out of corporate existence, but they'll leave voluntarily—they'll exit because they're discouraged by all the downsizing, worried that they might be next, and fed up with the increased workload. This knowledge drain will fuel the entrepreneurial revolution—a rise in small, risk-taking companies carving out profitable niches.

Big companies will need to reacquire some of that knowledge, and entrepreneurial companies will need all the resources large organizations can provide. All sorts of synergies will emerge, and Power of Two alliances will capitalize on them. These alliances are geared toward equal partnerships, and there will be an equality of need if not of size in the future—big companies will need their smaller partners as much as the smaller ones need big partners. The Power of Two provides a process for these diverse partners to work together.

Trend No. 2

The Internet and Such Will Facilitate Fast, Flexible Partnering

The expansion of the Internet as well as Extranet and Intranet sites is a great leveler. In cyberspace everyone is equal. Or, rather, everyone is only as big as their ideas and information. As organizations become accustomed to exchanging knowledge and doing business electronically, they'll also find themselves relying on their computer screen to research and explore new opportunities. And opportunities will be everywhere. A Power of Two mind-set will help companies be more open about prospective partners they encounter on the Web; it will help them prioritize the opportunity rather than the partner (its size, "name," and the like). We anticipate alliances where the partners never meet, where one company is located in Iowa and the other in South Korea, where trust is built through a knowledge exchange and organizations target purely electronic opportunities—they join forces to develop a web site for a mutual customer. Virtual companies will emerge and enter into alliances—alliances with Power of Two characteristics. Because of the nature of the medium—because the virtual company can move faster and more flexibly without physical baggage—they'll require strong relationships to capitalize on the medium. Power of Two alliances offer a process for building trust between alliance champions; trust is what will allow the alliance to move at the fastest modem speed available.

Trend No. 3

Super Champions

We're going to see the emergence of people who are brilliant alliance matchmakers, alliance champions who are so proficient at what they do that they can spot a perfect Power of Two match from a mile away. In our work, we've seen champions grow into their roles and become very astute about how to partner after they've gone through a number of alliances. The new business superstars will come from this champion group; the people on covers of Fortune and Forbes will be individuals who are skilled at building trusting relationships, seeing opportunities that won't emerge for years, and bringing organizations together to prepare for those opportunities.

Someone like Robert Campbell has almost a sixth sense about who would make a good partner. Campbell is the economic development director in Vista, California. He's created an economic growth boom in his town by matchmaking a variety of Power of Two alliances. For instance, a local tool-and-die manufacturer was operating at only 75 percent capacity. Campbell came across another organization that needed a fresh manufacturing source because of an increase in business. He intuitively recognized the match. The step-by-step process we've outlined in this book for finding a Power of Two ally is something Campbell can do instantly (or so it seems to us). As a veteran alliance maker and manager, he can analyze two companies with astonishing speed and judge if they would enjoy a productive partnership.

Trend No. 4

Branching Networks

Alliance networks are already rising quickly, and we're going to see many more of them in the future. These networks are designed to share resources and costs. Lean organizations are currently using business networks to replace what they've lost. Soon they'll realize that they can also be used to unearth and explore new opportunities. Lotus Development, for instance, is now interconnecting its alliance partners to conduct joint seminars, do co-op advertising, and to carry out joint selling. On the Internet you'll find companies establishing document links to many other companies. These loosely linked networks are going to grow like crazy. They'll grow not only because they can supply each other with missing resources and achieve economies of scale but because they can provide each other with a variety of terrific alliance partners to choose from. When that first glimmer of an opportunity touches the horizon, companies can search their network for the partner that is best able to help them pursue it. Instead of wasting time searching all over creation for that perfect partner, it's simply a matter of reviewing the qualifications of the ten or fifteen companies in your network.

Trend No. 5

A New Type of Training

The current vogue of team training will give way to alliance training. As companies realize that their future success is tied to their alliance-making and management abilities, they'll train people in relevant skills. We believe that the skills that will be most important—the ones that will lead to dynamic, productive alliances—are those that alliance champions possess. If you'll recall, the traits that characterize champions are integrity, strategic thinking, planning ability, visionary ideas, communication, collaborative capabilities, and persistence. Organizations will select and train their alliance representatives based on these seven traits. Instead of searching the organization for the best salespeople (which is how many organizations currently choose their relationship managers), management will develop a selection process and training curriculums built around a champion's traits.

Trend No. 6

Knowledge Sharing Becomes a Virtual Reality

Right now many organizations give lip service to knowledge exchanges. They may even hold knowledge-sharing sessions with partners in order to transfer information. But it's still a forced, formal activity; it only happens sporadically and with some trepidation. Two organizations are partnering today on a project that regularly hold sessions where they feed each other data related to a technology they're developing together. Before these sessions, however, management censors the data and only allows some of it to pass on to the partner.

In the coming years we're going to see the knowledge gates open wide. For one thing, it's going to be much easier to exchange knowledge as Internet sites provide forums for doing so; it's likely that a great amount of software will be developed specifically for this purpose—software that organizes the knowledge and disseminates it to the right people within a network.

Organizations are also going to start believing what everyone has been saying: that knowledge really is a competitive edge. We're moving toward parity in so many areas—in our technology, our products, our services, our pricing—that one of the few differentiators remaining is what you know that others don't. No organization—no matter how big or how smart—knows as much as two organizations (or as much as an alliance network). Every company is limited by its experiences and perspectives; another company brings fresh experiences and perspectives. If it's the right combination of companies, not only do you have more knowledge at your disposal but you also have a way to spark more and better ideas.

Power of Two alliances provide companies with a secure method of exchanging knowledge. The trust developed by champions, the rules of engagement, and the linkage between knowledge and co-creating opportunities all provide incentives and pathways for knowledge to be exchanged.

Trend No. 7

Disappearing Boundaries

The traditional definition of what constitutes a corporation is changing quickly. As companies outsource, lease, and form various types of alliances, the lines blur between one company and the next. In the near future, we suspect that the largest corporations will make twenty-five or even fifty alliances within the course of a year. They'll enter into so many partnerships that it will be difficult to view a company as a single entity. Instead it will be more like an amoeba, forming and re-forming itself continuously.

Gone too will be the boundaries between competitors, domestic and foreign markets, and customer and supplier. Even internally, the rise of cross-functional teams has shattered boundaries. What all this means is that traditional partnerships will go the way of the dodo bird. It will be difficult for Company A to acquire Company B when one or both companies has scores of alliances—even the thought of such an acquisition would give a corporate lawyer nightmares for months.

Power of Two alliances are well suited to a boundary-less world. They don't lock in on a partnership and attempt to milk it for the year; they don't dictate that you can only partner with a certain type of company in a certain location. Champions look for partners that are best able to help their organizations go after opportunities at a given point in time; other considerations are of only tangential concern. The alliance champions we've worked with are already able to ignore many of the boundaries that divide one company from another and pursue a partnership as if those boundaries didn't exist.

Trend No. 8

The Short-Term, Long-Term Paradox

Currently there's an emphasis on meeting quarterly numbers, but this short-term thinking is gradually being balanced by a concern with long-term goals. There's a growing realization that it will be much easier to meet those quarterly requirements in the future if companies are prepared for the opportunities that come their way.

More and more we're hearing companies saying things like, "I'm going to need 40 percent more capacity to build my widgets three or four years from now." Combining technologically sophisticated forecasting tools with visionary thinking, organizations are starting to look longer, harder, and more accurately into their crystal balls. Though they still worry about what the analysts are going to think of their quarterly results, they also worry about whether they'll be prepared to pounce on an opportunity four years from now.

Partnering for possible future business opportunities is Power of Two thinking. Developing the knowledge, technologies, and other resources to position yourself properly when a new market emerges is what drives many of the best alliances. It's not that alliances don't want to make short-term profits; it's that they know that to make those profits in the future, they have to get a big head start through partnering today.

Trend No. 9

Reexamining Relationships

Over the next decade we're going to see many companies seriously rethinking their traditional relationships. To a certain extent we've already seen that happening as companies put their vendors to quality and other tests and attempt to form true partnerships with suppliers. But this reexamination is going to be much more extensive in coming years. When companies outsource one function successfully, they stop and think, "Maybe we should take the next step." The next step may mean more outsourcing. Or it may mean exploring other partnering options. We've found that when organizations establish one successful Power of Two alliance it opens their eyes to the alliance possibilities. Management often wonders: "Have we been limiting ourselves by only collaborating with a few different companies?"

The answer, of course, is yes. In the past, organizations established long-term relationships with an ad agency, a few suppliers, a consulting firm, an accounting firm. They exposed themselves to the same type of thinking year in and year out. Power of Two alliances are always reexamining relationships; they're always searching for and analyzing other partnerships. An alliance is not like a marriage; one partner is not being unfaithful to the other by saying "this isn't working anymore" and looking for someone else. In the world of business relationships (as opposed to the world of emotional ones), blind fidelity will destroy you.

Trend No. 10

From Transaction-Based to Relationship-Based

Consider how the banking business has evolved. It has gone from a transaction-based strategy to a relationship-driven one. Financial institutions have recognized that customers want more than the best rates or nice premiums for opening accounts. What they want is service—personalized, value-added service. Developing relationships with banking customers is what will keep them customers, even if the bank down the block offers a little better rate. After all, rates fluctuate, good relationships don't.

This trend is influencing how organizations view alliances. They're recognizing that transaction-based alliances are flimsy and narrowly focused, and that relationship-based alliances are strong and visionary. The relationship bond between alliance champions is central to Power of Two alliances. It's this relationship far more than anything else that draws two companies together and keeps them focused and moving toward challenging goals.

The Power of Two to the Nth Degree

We'd like to leave you with the image of chameleon-like corporations, constantly changing to fit in with a changing environment. You can already glimpse this type of company in the way organizations are launching various change initiatives, restructuring their work forces, and making other transformational moves. But this process is going to greatly accelerate in the future, and the only way companies can keep up is by becoming alliance masters.

Right now alliances are a relatively small component of most companies' business strategies (if they exist at all). In the future they will be at the organizational core. Every day will bring new alliance possibilities; partnerships will be formed, ended, and reformed regularly; alliances will transcend geographical, cultural, and other borders. It's not hard to imagine an alliance war room where maps of alliance partners and prospects are kept in the form of an alliance network, where partnering moves are plotted out in advance of changes to the business strategy. For big companies as well as small ones, the business of alliance formation and management can become very complex.

The Power of Two offers a process to manage that complexity. We don't claim that it's a perfect process. In fact, it's probably in its infancy, and we expect to get the bugs out and improve it as we learn more about how and why alliances work. For now, however, it's the best tool we've found for establishing strong, effective partnerships. And it's a tool that we feel will become even more powerful as alliances become a way of life, as champions multiply, and as top managers embrace this new way of conducting business.

Index